# FACES IN A MIRROR

# FACES IN A MIRROR

## Memoirs from Exile

## Ashraf Pahlavi

PRENTICE-HALL, INC., Englewood Cliffs, N.J.

Address inquiries to Prentice-Hall, Inc.,
Englewood Cliffs, N.J. 07632
Printed in the United States of America
Prentice-Hall International, Inc., London
Prentice-Hall of Australia, Pty. Ltd., Sydney
Prentice-Hall of Canada, Ltd., Toronto
Prentice-Hall of India Private Ltd., New Delhi
Prentice-Hall of Japan, Inc., Tokyo
Prentice-Hall of Southeast Asia Pte. Ltd., Singapore
Whitehall Books Limited, Wellington, New Zealand

10 9 8 7 6 5 4 3 2

**Library of Congress Cataloging in Publication Data**
Ashraf, Princess of Iran, 1919-
Faces in a mirror.
Includes index.
1. Ashraf, Princess of Iran, 1919- 2. Iran—
Princes and princesses—Biography. 3. Iran—History—
Mohammed Reza Pahlavi, 1941-1979. I. Title.
DS318.A85  955'.053'0924  80-13509
ISBN 0-13-299131-4

*To my son Shahriar—*
*and to those like him who*
*fell in the name of Iran*

# CONTENTS

# INTRODUCTION

I write these memoirs from exile—from New York where I have been in virtual seclusion since the "revolution" in Iran of February 1979. The windows from where I write overlook the East River and have a clear view of the United Nations. I had worked there for 16 years: as one of the delegates from Iran, as a member of the Human Rights Commission, later as Chairman of the Human Rights Commission, and, for seven years, as head of the Iranian delegation. So, of course, I know the UN well, as a kind of "second home." I cherished the countless hours spent there and came to believe that this forum, above most others, could be counted on to be honorable in its debate of the issues brought before it. How hard it is for me then—and to be candid, how bitter it leaves me—to have to watch from the outside as those who were on record as my friends now sanction the formation of the UN Commission to hear the chorus of attacks against the Iran of the Pahlavis.

By now I should be hardened to such attacks, there have been so many in this year of rapidly changing events. But in truth I am not, and I have tried to understand—as one always does in time of shock and grief and sorrow—exactly what has happened to Iran and to my twin brother, the Shah. I have had long talks with him (since childhood he has been the one source of consolation for me in times of trouble) about the causes of this turmoil. We discussed the ways in which he—following the lead of my father, Reza Shah—tried to transform Iran from a backward, medieval culture into a strong and unified modern nation. I have reflected on the means—and on the speed—with which this vision was implemented, and it is clear that ours has been a story of achievements and mistakes. But it is equally clear to me now that it is a story that must include the role of the West and that the West, too, has not fully understood its own mistakes and its own achievements in Iran.

This failure of understanding led many Western nations, America in particular, to assume that if the Shah was removed the path would be clear for "instant" democracy. (Yet any student of Iranian psychology might have predicted that the displacement of the Shah would result in the emergence of another strong father figure—one such as Ruhollah Khomeini.) And it was on the basis of this assumption, which I can only consider to have been pure fantasy, that the Carter Administration—in its betrayal of the Shah— unleashed on Iran, on itself, and on the rest of the world one of the most serious political crises since the end of World War II. (For America must know by now that the fall of the Shah has had, and will continue to have, dire consequences and has dangerously upset the world's balance of power.)

How farfetched this fantasy was, I think, is dramatically illustrated by the blatant tyranny of Khomeini's regime: by its bloody purges; by its repression of women; by the flight of one and a half million Iranians, including most of the country's intellectuals and professionals; by the seizure of the U.S. Embassy and the holding of fifty Americans as hostage. I think all of these events must be causing a great deal of bewilderment, as well as consternation, in official circles no less than among the American public. And I wonder most of all what those in the American administration make of the vehement anti-American (and anti-Carter) denunciations with which Khomeini repays them for their support.

The last time I saw Iran was in August 1978. I had returned from a conference of the World Health Organization in Russia and found the country in the midst of mounting disorder. My brother urged me to leave, which I did, and I watched from a distance as Iran moved closer and closer to total upheaval. Then in January 1979, when my brother himself left Teheran, I shared his despair as he was forced into exile, as the man whose life has been so inextricably intertwined with mine had to search for a new home. It was a search that began in Aswan, took him next to Morocco, then to the Bahamas, to Cuernevaca, to a New York hospital room, to an American Air Force base in Texas, and, finally, to Panama. I have tried to lighten the burden of this troubled time for him, to be there when I could, to share the difficulties of his exile and his illness.

I remember how, in the cold isolation of a hospital room, we spent his sixtieth birthday (or, I should say, *our* sixtieth birthday), with the encouragement inside of thousands of letters of support—while, outside, the controversy raged about whether or not the American Government at least owed an ally of thirty-seven years access to proper medical treatment. This controversy escalated with the seizure of the American Embassy in Teheran, along with the fifty hostages, and the demand of a ransom that was nothing less than the right to dictate American policy.

And now I have seen this ransom paid, in installments, first as America's politicians rushed to dissociate themselves from a ruler they had praised and supported for decades, then as they joined their voices in a concert of "mea culpas" for having given him this support. Finally, there came a kind of uneasy silence, which no doubt seemed the easiest way of all for dealing with the unpalatable realities of how America treats her former allies and what her own role was in bringing about the current chaos in Iran.

For me, the greatest anxieties in this time have been related to my brother's health, to the isolation, and to the dangerous threats he and his family have had to face. The last time I saw him was in February 1980, when I flew by small plane to the Panamanian resort island of Contadora. As we landed on an elevated airstrip I could, through the coconut trees, see the ocean, and I was glad that my brother, who has lived this year under a kind of siege, had at least this vista and the illusion of freedom it creates. The island has a hotel complex and a number of private villas. It is in one of these that my brother now lives—a four bedroom, two-story house with a peaked roof of yellow tiles. The island has a six-month rainy season, but when I made my visit, the weather was dry, so my brother and I took long walks, as we had in childhood, and we talked, though now about the harsher circumstances of our adult world.

During the first of these walks, I was struck by how remarkably unembittered my brother is about his treatment by a country with whose leaders he had the closest ties. Yet he sees, as I do, how serious and how deep the gap has been between America and Iran. Iran's growing unrest in the late 1970's was a complicated historical, social, economic phenomenon. Yet America interpreted this opposition to the throne as a call for a more Westernized form of government. In doing so, I think it failed to comprehend the enormous differences between our cultures, particularly the historic roots of the monarchy in a society where children for centuries have learned the words for "God-Country-Shah" as indivisible.

On another walk, my brother and I talked about how we

have been at a loss to explain America's response to the Khomeini regime—the response to acts of piracy and terrorism with a policy that appears to be basically one of appeasement. Understandably, the hostage situation necessitated restraint. But in its attitude and actions, the American Government has provided a lesson that will not be lost on other unfriendly countries: namely that acts of piracy and terrorism may well be the negotiating tools of the future, the means by which weaker nations can "equalize" the gap between their own power and that of the United States.

This mood of appeasement has, of course, touched the Pahlavis personally since the United States now acquiesces in having its Iranian policy, along with charges against the Shah, investigated by the UN Commission—the final bit of ransom paid to the "old man from Qum." The creation of this Commission has been most disillusioning to me, since it has been the work of Secretary-General Kurt Waldheim, a man who was my friend and associate during the last seven years at the UN. Try as I may, I cannot understand this kind of reversal, for while political betrayals are almost a fact of daily life in our part of the world, I had perhaps naive expectations of something else and something more from the UN and from the United States. I had not expected them to embark on such an unprecedented and questionable course—the selection of those who represent themselves as qualified to sit in judgment on the political history of a nation. And who then, I wonder, will judge these judges?

This is only one of the questions that has occurred to me in this last year of exile. Since the summer of 1979, I have been putting down my thoughts and reflections, spending five or six hours a day trying to reconstruct from memory (since the revolution, most of my personal documents have been burned in Teheran) the story of Iran under the Pahlavis. I have done this partly because I am a woman who cannot be without work, and I felt compelled to find a way to fill the hours. I also felt the need to record events as I saw them— and from the inside as only I could know them. I began to search my memory for details of the Persia of my childhood, the Persia of veiled women and ancient bazaars. I started to recall scenes of war-torn Iran—the dust clouds that rose as the Allied trucks took over our roads. I remember the Teheran Conference. I remember my first visit to Stalin at the start of the cold war when Iran was facing grave dangers from the Soviet Union and from the threat of Communism. I began to reconstruct my intense personal struggle with one of Iran's strongest and most controversial Prime Ministers, Mohammed Mossadegh. I also remembered, and have de- cided to reveal, my instrumental role in "Operation Ajax"— the C.I.A. operation that led to Mossadegh's fall and kept Iran from the hands of the Communists.

But as I began to work, and as the months passed, I felt also a certain urgency to go on, as I read countless distor- tions from all quarters as to what had happened in Iran during my brother's reign. I saw unsubstantiated allegations of widespread tortures and killings by SAVAK; undocu- mented charges of financial mismanagement and theft; un- documented accusations of wholesale repression. I realized that these allegations were displacing the truth, that the pages of *Faces in a Mirror* might well be the only place where the public will be able to read the story of the Pahlavis as I have seen it and as I have lived it.

Some of my friends have cautioned me, told me that silence on my part would be the most politic attitude—since the current regime in Iran now speaks for itself. For many months, I was silent, as my brother's search for a home and the seizure of the hostages created a world situation that might have made it irresponsible to say anything at all. But now, as I watch not only the tragedies in Iran, but also the sham of the UN Commission I feel I must speak—which is more in keeping with my personality.

Two decades ago French journalists named me "La Panthère Noire" ("The Black Panther"), and I must admit that I rather like that name, and that, in some respects, it suits me. Like the panther, my nature is turbulent, rebellious, self-confident. Often, it is only through strenuous effort that I maintain my reserve and my composure in public. But in truth, I sometimes wish I were armed with the panther's claws so that I might attack the enemies of my country. I know that these enemies—and particularly in the light of recent events—have characterized me as ruthless and unforgiving; almost a reincarnation of the devil himself. My detractors have accused me of being a smuggler, a spy, a Mafia associate (once even a drug dealer), and an agent of all intelligence and counterintelligence agencies in the world.

It is in part such allegations that have also led me to write this book—not as a way of defending myself, but as a way of considering these charges candidly and truthfully, and as a way of setting out the political events in my country, as well as the events of my personal life. But beyond this, I want very much to explain to Western readers what they have failed to understand about the nature of Iran's culture and heritage, about the diversity and factionalism that now threaten to disintegrate the country, about the nature of the so-called Islamic revival, about the opposition the Pahlavis unleashed when they took the West as their model of progress and change, and about the violently anti-Western sentiment so prevalent throughout the Middle East right now.

All of this I can discuss now in a way that perhaps I never could before. Now the members of my family are in exile, scattered all over the world—except for one. On a cold December day in 1979, my daughter Azadeh phoned to tell me that my son Shahriar had been shot and killed in a Paris street. My grief was that of any mother who has lost a child, but my sadness was for my son, who had been a soldier, a Commander in Iran's navy, who, although he left his country after the revolution told me that he could not bear to live his life in exile. And though he is gone, I could not bring myself to bury him in a foreign land. I have had his body embalmed—and I promise that one day he will be buried in his own country.

So now, with little more left to lose, I can tell the story of who I am and what the Pahlavis—my father and, of course, my brother—have meant to me and to Iran.

Ashraf Pahlavi
New York, March 1980

# FACES
# IN A
# MIRROR

# · I ·

# REZA KHAN

I can picture him as he must have been then, a tall giant of a man—intense, volatile, fired by restless energy—pacing around the pool in the brick courtyard of our house, smoking the Persian cigarettes he craved so much. Flanked by the men of his brigade, he waited on that chilly autumn day of October 26, 1919. Three years earlier my sister Shams had been born, and now Reza Khan Pahlavi, Commander of the Persian Cossack Brigade, had to have a son.

The tension broke when one of his soldiers ran into the courtyard: "It's a boy!"

But when my father rushed toward the house to see the child who was his heir, he was stopped by the midwife who attended my mother in her confinement.

"Wait. There is another child."

Arriving five hours later, I generated none of the excitement that greeted my brother's birth. To say that I was unwanted might be harsh, but not altogether far from the truth. There was already my adored sister Shams, and now a son who embodied the fulfillment of my parents' dreams. To be born on the same day as Mohammed Reza Pahlavi, future Crown Prince and then Shah of Iran, I would always feel I could lay no claim to my parents' special affection.

Yet it was this twinship and this relationship with my brother that would nourish and sustain me throughout my childhood, that would constitute the strongest sense of family that I would ever know. No matter how I would reach out in the years to come—sometimes even desperately—to find an identity and a purpose of my own, I would remain inextricably tied to my twin brother. I would marry more than once. I would have children of my own. I would work for my country in ways unheard of for a woman of my generation. I would even go into exile (three times) alone. But always the center of my existence was, and is, Mohammed Reza Pahlavi.

At the time my brother and I were born, Reza Khan had already cast a giant shadow over the political scene in Persia, one that extended far from the northern mountain village of Alasht (not far from the Russian border) where he had been born in 1876. His father, an army officer, had died when my father was still an infant, leaving my grandmother with no means of her own. In those days a young woman in this position suffered severe hardships when her husband died, for without his protection, she became, for all practical purposes, the ward of her in-laws.

Strong-willed as I have heard she was, my grandmother wanted to raise her child on her own terms, and she decided to leave Alasht and return to her native Teheran. Her infant son in her arms, she crossed the mountains on foot, following the caravans to the capital, where she found comfort in the company of her own family and friends.

My father rarely discussed his childhood, but from what little he did say, I know that because of the death of his father, and because his mother refused to be dominated by her in-laws (a refusal which cut her off from their financial assistance), he grew up in an atmosphere of hardship which toughened him and taught him the value of self-reliance. At that time only the very rich could afford a formal education, and since my grandfather had been a military man before his death, my father grew up with the idea of becoming a soldier. It was a good choice, because he was exceptionally tall and strong, even for the northern mountain regions, which are known to have the tallest men in Iran.

By the time he reached the age of 16, he was over six feet tall and still growing. He enlisted in the Persian Cossack Brigade (the Persians, like the Russians, use the word "cossack" for soldier), a crack military unit which represented the only "modern" (by Persian standards) fighting force in the country.

From the very beginning of his military career, I think it was clear to those who knew Reza Khan that he was destined for something other than the life of an ordinary soldier. In his fur hat and leather boots, astride a spirited horse, he was an imposing figure, but more than that, he had a flair for the kind of heroic feats and daring that create military legends. With experience he would become a first-rate tactician and a disciplined front-line fighter; but if these had been his only skills, he might have become a competent general and nothing more.

That he went further was the result of his intuitive grasp of battlefield psychology and the willingness to risk his life in bold theatrical strokes that would create an aura of invincibility and win the unquestioning loyalty of his men. On more than one occasion he left his troops on the fringes of a battle site and rode alone, unarmed, into the territory of a dissident tribal chief, a gesture that more than once led to a bloodless victory.

From a historical perspective, it can be said that a man like Reza Khan was long overdue on Persia's political scene. To understand this is to understand the conditions in Persia at the beginning of the twentieth century. It is to understand Persia's economic poverty, its vulnerability to foreign inter-

3

vention, and its position at the center of the Islamic world. These basic realities, which I believe the West still has not understood, dominate our history even today. Unlike Europe to the west, the Persia of 80 years ago had reached one of its most serious declines in 2,500 years. (Only the decline in the second half of the eighteenth century had been worse.) From the highly developed civilizations of Cyrus and Darius, it had become an impoverished country, ruled by the tired and politically bankrupt Qajar dynasty. Its enormous land mass—1,648,000 square kilometers—was divided into ten provinces, unconnected by either roads or a communications system to the seat of government in Teheran. Sometimes one even had to travel through a foreign country to reach one of our own provinces. To reach Khuzestan, it was necessary to go by way of Iraq; to get to Khorrasan, it was necessary to go through Russia.

Except for the clusters of merchants and artisans in Teheran, Tabriz, and other cities, Persia was an agricultural country of huge estates where tenant farmers lived and worked in abject poverty under a feudal system that benefited the landlords (often called "the thousand families"). Nomadic tribes kept flocks of sheep and goats, following the seasons, as their ancestors had done for hundreds of years. Although the existence of oil was known for centuries, Persia never had the funds or the expertise to develop this resource. Ours was a primitive medieval country, with no paved roads, no sanitation, no postal service, no school system, and no hospitals, a country where 98 percent of the population was illiterate and where women had virtually no civil rights. Life expectancy was 30 years and infant mortality was one of the highest in the world.

Effective political power was in the hands of landlords and tribal chieftains (each of whom had a standing army), who also operated within a primitive system, exercising complete control over their own people. In a sense, this was a country of provincial states. The king, Nasr-ed-din-Shah

4

(1848–96), had become a figurehead to whom the tribal leaders tendered only token respect. His actual position might be illustrated by the methods used for the collection of taxes. Although these were theoretically to be paid directly to the royal treasury, the king in fact had no power to enforce these collections. It was the chieftains who, with their armed followers, would serve as "collection agencies," but not before taking a substantial percentage for their services. The royal treasury was often bare, and it was not unheard of for the government to borrow money from the merchants of the Teheran bazaars.

This weakened state and the absence of a strong central government and effective army made Persia continually vulnerable to foreign intervention and interference. If we are to fathom the mood of Iran today, we must remember that although Persia was never colonized, it was regularly invaded and infiltrated by forces more sophisticated and powerful than its own.

To Russia on the north, Persia represented, as it still does, 1,800 kilometers of common frontier and vital access to warm water ports. To Britain, Persia offered untapped natural resources—particularly oil, which would become the lifeblood of the industrialized West—and a logical geopolitical extension of its vast colonial empire in Asia and Africa. Each of these powers made alliances with individual tribal leaders, and through them, Britain and Russia exercised their spheres of influence, backing them with armed force when necessary.

All of this—Persia's economic insolvency and its vulnerability to foreign interference—must be seen against a background of Islamic tradition still in the Dark Ages. Although Islam does recognize the division between secular and spiritual matters, the Shi'ite clergy (the *mullahs*), representing the state religion of Persia, have generally been more politically active than their Sunni counterparts, who represent the dominant majority in such countries as Egypt,

Oman, Qatar, and Kuwait. Many influential clergymen formed alliances with representatives of foreign powers, most often the British, and there was, in fact, a standing joke in Persia that said if you picked up a clergyman's beard, you would see the words "Made in England" stamped on the other side.

These Shi'ite mullahs exercised a powerful influence over the minds of the masses. In the rural villages the mullah was often the only man who could read and write. To the peasant, he was scribe and teacher, the man who could interpret the voice of God and hold out promises of Paradise. And if at times the voice of God seemed to be speaking with a British or Russian accent, it was difficult for the peasant to decipher where religion left off and politics began.

Given this state of affairs and the frustrations of trying to rule an impoverished country of some 10 million people, Nasr-ed-din-Shah preferred to spend his time in the more cultivated capitals of Europe. When his funds ran low, he would look to the British and the Russians, who gladly accommodated him, in return for a series of concessions which virtually mortgaged Persia's resources. By the time he was assassinated in 1896, Nasr-ed-din-Shah had turned over the country's fisheries (caviar) to the Russians—and made a series of other concessions to the British.

This pattern continued under his son, Mozzafar-ed-din-Shah, who in 1901, signed over the oil rights in southern Persia to the English entrepreneur, William Knox D'Arcy, for 20,000 pounds. This agreement, and others that followed, would become the focus of bitter political struggles, not only with the British, but within Persia itself. The entire history of Persia up to the revolution itself and the current crisis cannot be separated from the history of oil.

A turning point, a reaction against this foreign exploitation, came with the development of an embryonic "Young Persians" movement, aimed at establishing a constitutional government and ridding the country of outside influences.

This motif—first of alliance, then of reaction, revulsion, and disenchantment with the world outside—is a familiar one in the tapestry of Middle Eastern politics, one that has appeared as it does today with almost cyclical regularity.

The Constitutionalists were particularly strong in Tabriz, the capital of Azerbaijan, the province closest to Russia and Turkey, where in the early 1900's a well-developed "Young Turks" movement sought to end the Caliphate and foreign intervention and establish a republic.

What happened was that the Russian Tsar, not wishing to see the spread of any Constitutional movement on his borders, supported the Qajar Shah. He sent Russian officers to train and command the Cossack Brigade and to ensure its loyalty to the throne. The British supported the Constitutionalists, who in 1906 were victorious when they forced the king to accept a National Assembly. Two years later the Russians ordered the Cossack Brigade to back the king, Mohammed Ali Shah, when he dissolved the Assembly and arrested the "Young Persians." This is the kind of political check and checkmate that was being played in Persia when World War I broke out. It reinforced the prevailing feeling of the people that everything that happens in Persia is the result of foreign intervention (a feeling which is perhaps stronger today than ever before).

During the war years Persia declared its neutrality, but our borders were violated by the Russians, the British, and the Turks, who waged some of their bloodiest battles on Persian soil, often not differentiating between civilian populations and enemy soldiers. After five years of war, Persia and its people were debilitated and demoralized, the national mood one of despair.

In August 1919, two months before I was born, the Qajar Shah reluctantly signed a treaty with England granting Persia assistance and arms in return for a continued British presence through technical and military advisers. The Russians, as an outgrowth of the revolution, had started to spread the seeds of bolshevism in one of the northern provinces along the Caspian Sea. In the capital there was agitation against the British and their treaty. The demand for the king's abdication became more and more vocal.

My father had never been an avidly political man (even after he became king, he referred to himself as a simple soldier). All his energies had been devoted to improving his military skills, and indeed, he had risen rapidly through the ranks of the Cossack Brigade. But he had begun to wonder why his unit took its orders from Russian officers and why it had been sent to suppress the patriotism of the Constitutionalists. He later watched the nationalistic struggle in Turkey, where Mustafa Kemal (later known as Ataturk), a military man like himself, was creating a new nation out of a ruined country nicknamed "the sick man of Europe."

As soon as he had established enough of a personal power base and earned the unquestioning loyalty of his men, Reza Khan purged his unit of its Russian officers. In February 1921, in a well-planned and finely executed bloodless coup, my father led 2,000 Cossacks into Teheran and established his personal control over the city. Ahmad Shah, who succeeded Mohammed Ali Shah, was still nominally king; but my father, as Commander-in-Chief of the army and Minister of War, became the ruling force in the Teheran government, and in 1923 he became Prime Minister.

The final consolidation of his power came when he led his army against the powerful tribes of the oil-rich province of Khuzistan and brought them under his authority. In 1925 a Constituent Assembly proclaimed the end of the 131-year-old Qajar dynasty.

Now Persia (the country was not called Iran until 1935) had to decide what form of government it would adopt. My father favored a republic, like that of Turkey, and he proposed this idea to the leading Shi'ite mullahs. But at a meeting in the holy city of Qum, the clergy—staunch supporters of the feudal system, the monarchy, and all tradition representing the status quo—told my father they would

oppose any plan for a republic. So Reza Khan was proclaimed Shah of Persia on December 17, 1925. My brother and
I were six years old.

Reza Shah was now the most powerful man in Persia. The
same qualities that made him a formidable soldier—piercing
eyes that could wither a subordinate, intolerance for error
and imperfection, insistence on strict military discipline—
also made him an awesome and frightening father. Whenever I saw a trouser leg with a red stripe approaching, I
would run, on the theory that the best way to avoid my
father's displeasure was to stay out of his way.

Looking back, I can't think of a single instance when my
father punished any of us, but his physical presence to us as
children was so intimidating, the sound of his voice raised in
anger so terrifying, that even years later as a grown woman I
can't remember a time when I wasn't afraid of him.

My mother, Taj-ol-Muluk, presented a striking physical
contrast to my father. A small delicate woman with blond
hair and beautiful green eyes, she barely reached the top row
of military decorations on my father's uniform. Yet in her
own way, she was as forceful as he was. At a time when
Iranian women were veiled and "hidden," when they had
virtually no rights, when they were expected to submit
totally to male authority, my mother wasn't afraid to argue
with my father or to challenge his decisions.

My father and my mother's brother had been soldiers
together in the Cossack Brigade, and they had arranged the
marriage in traditional Persian fashion, without any real
contact between bride and groom before the wedding. At a
time when teenage brides were customary, my mother was
married at 24. In later years my father would tease her,
saying: "You know, you were really very lucky to find a
husband at such an old age."

"No, no," she would always protest. "You're quite
wrong. I was only eighteen."

When my brother and I were still very young and my

9

mother pregnant with our brother Ali Reza, my father took another wife, a much younger woman. (Actually my father had been married at the age of 17 to a cousin, Maryam Khanum, who had died giving birth to a daughter, Ham-dam-os-Saltaneh.) Although polygamy was commonly practiced (Islamic law allowed as many as four wives), and although women were expected to accept this condition, my mother was very angry. For a long time she refused to see my father. In the face of this unheard of challenge to his authority, the Shah would literally hide when he saw my mother coming. Remembering this, I think I must have been influenced by the examples of strength she set in a society where women were expected neither to be seen nor heard.

Eventually my parents did reach an understanding. With his second wife, my father had a son, and with still another wife there were five more children. Although we were 11 children in all, there was, in accord with my mother's wishes, very little mixing among the children of the three marriages (in later years, however, many of us would become friends). My mother would be the official queen, my brother the heir to the throne. The other families lived separately, in other quarters inside the palace.

Although my family was large, my childhood was often lonely. As the first child, Shams was the favorite daughter. As the first son and Crown Prince, my brother was, of course, cherished by everyone. I realized very early that I was an outsider, that I would have to create a place for myself. In later years my critics would say I had overdone this somewhat, that my presence was everywhere. But as a child I was scarcely noticed at all.

My female companions were my *nanneh*, a peasant woman from Shahristanak, and a blind woman (whose niece still lives with me) who would tell me bedtime stories. She would spin stories of kings whose sons were mysteriously ill, or of kings with three beautiful daughters—traditional fairy tales that brought a touch of color and romance into the strict atmosphere of our daily routine.

Isolated as I felt, I don't believe I often thought of myself as a royal princess; the reality that I was came briefly to life on the day of my father's coronation. My nanny and I were standing in the midst of a large and noisy crowd. As a splendid carriage pulled by white horses passed, I saw my father inside, a jewel-studded crown on his head. Cries of "Long live the king" filled the streets, and I was carried along with an excitement I didn't quite understand.

Soon after that we moved to an annex of the Golestan Palace, the Palace of Roses, which had been completed by Fath Ali Shah Qajar in 1806 to house some of the two thousand children and grandchildren he sired. My father refused to actually live there, though he did spend the day in the palace conducting official business. For him, it was tainted with the ignominious history of the Qajars and a not very glorious past. He would build his own palace—the Marble Palace, which would be completed in time for my brother's wedding celebration in 1938—about 3 kilometers from Golestan, in what is now midtown Teheran. In the meantime, he would sleep in a small and very simple house not far from the palace. He may have been king, and now he certainly had the means to enjoy a more lavish mode of living, but Reza Shah still preferred a military lifestyle of almost Spartan simplicity. He often slept on the floor, allowing himself only one small luxury—a silver cigarette case.

For us children, those first few days of royalty were spent exploring the lush gardens of cypress and pine, the great halls with their huge wall frescoes, and ceilings of mosaic mirrors that glittered like diamonds.

In the official part of the palace was the Marble Throne, on which my father had been crowned, as well as the world-famous Peacock Throne, a magnificent golden armchair encrusted with diamonds, rubies, and other precious stones. That throne, along with a number of other precious objects, had been brought to Persia from India 240 years ago by Nadir Shah, a Persian precursor of Napoleon Bonaparte.

As soon as we settled into our new quarters, Reza Shah let us know there would be no more frivolity. I was to call my brother "Your Highness," and he was to prepare himself for the responsibilities ahead. I doubt that I understood exactly what "Your Highness" meant, but I knew this was another way in which my brother was set apart from the rest of us.

With my mother, my sister, and my nanny, I lived in the palace's *andarun*, the women's quarters, in a section that had been occupied by the Qajar king's favorite concubine. Our rooms were not sumptuous by any means, but they were, by European standards, pleasant and comfortable, furnished with souvenirs of the Qajar kings' European visits—Venetian glass chandeliers, French vases, and French-style furniture. My brother lived in another set of rooms, which also housed his tutor, his bodyguard, and the other men in his entourage.

Unlike Shams, who was content to spend her day playing with dolls or following my mother around, I longed to be with my brother (sometimes I even ran away to play with him for an hour or two when I wasn't supposed to). But most of the time we were separated. He was tutored every morning with his friends, while Shams and I had our own lessons. As we grew older, though, I could often join him at 11:30—precisely—for lunch with our father. (When my brother Ali Reza was old enough, he, too, became part of this ritual.) This was a command performance, and if any of us had the bad luck to be late, we would stand outside the dining room, not daring to enter until we were given permission. Ironically, Ali Reza, the child who would grow up to most resemble my father, was the one who most often provoked Reza Shah's formidable temper by constantly breaking the punctuality rule.

Meals were simple and fairly predictable. The cook knew what foods my father liked and served them regularly. Rice, the Persian staple, was the basis for every meal. We might also have some soup and a small entree as well. Father's favorite dessert was pears. I never liked pears, but at our table the children weren't allowed to say, "I don't like this or that." To this day, I still hate pears.

Persian style eating was done with the hands, with bread used as a utensil. My father, however, leaning more toward the Western ways he associated with progress, wanted us to learn Western eating habits. We tried to follow all his rules, but sometimes we did behave like the children we were. Sometimes, when we thought he wasn't looking, we would start throwing flowers at each other across the table. Years later I realized that he only pretended not to notice.

Once Shams and I arrived for lunch only to be told by the servants: "You can't come in today. His Majesty is entertaining the King and Queen of Sweden and their daughter." Instead of leaving right away, Shams and I stood there, giggling. Suddenly the door opened and the guests started to come in. There was no place for us to go, so we hid in the passageway behind some partly closed curtains. At one point, Reza Shah walked right past us. We held our breath and stood as still as statues. Again, he pretended not to notice.

Occasionally my father would not only turn a blind eye to our lapses from military decorum, he would even join us. He and my brother made up a private code, which they would use to tell jokes and secrets when they didn't want anyone else to understand.

If we had known that underneath his stern and unyielding military exterior my father was capable of very tender feelings for us, we might have been happier children. But for me, the outward appearance always stood in the way of a comfortable and easy father-daughter relationship. Even as

13

an adult I would weigh my words carefully before I brought up any subject that might provoke or displease him.

Although I feared my father, I shared some of his qualities: his stubbornness, his fierce pride, and his iron will. If I wasn't given much attention, then I certainly wouldn't seek it. I remember some nights, when I couldn't sleep or when I woke up from a nightmare, I would tiptoe to the door of my mother's room, where I would see my mother and sister curled up together, fast asleep. I would cry a little outside the door, then go back to my nanny, convinced that there was no "special place" for me. I realized very early that I would have to learn to solve my own problems, to think and act independently, but not without paying a price.

My sister Shams and I never got along as children (though we did become good friends as adults), perhaps because we had very little in common. Shams was, like my mother, small and delicate and fair, very feminine and comfortable in the traditional female role, which was centered completely on marriage and homemaking. She loved to play with her hundreds of dolls and always looked forward to the day when she would have a husband and children of her own.

For me, the only companion who really mattered was my brother, and I literally lived for the time I could spend with him. I trusted him and confided in him, told him my secrets and asked his advice, and long before we reached adulthood, his voice became the dominant one in my life. I obeyed Reza Shah because I felt I had to, but I listened to my brother because I couldn't imagine doing anything else.

# FACES IN A MIRROR

Since I identified so strongly with my brother, I suppose I became what Americans call a tomboy. Whenever I could, I joined him and his friends, at riding horses or playing tennis and other athletic games. In a society where there was very little free mingling of the sexes, those years gave me an unusual sense of comfort and ease in the company of men. Even now, I still prefer the company of men to that of women.

As close as we were emotionally, my brother and I were very different in temperament and personality. He was gentle, reserved, and almost painfully shy, while I was volatile, quick-tempered, and sometimes rebellious. He was somewhat frail and vulnerable to every childhood disease, while I was robust and healthy, in spite of my small frame (all of us inherited my mother's physique). "I think you must have gotten all the good health," my father would joke.

You can imagine how painful this became when my brother was stricken with typhoid fever at the age of seven. There were no wonder drugs in 1926, and certainly Teheran had none of the medical facilities that existed in Europe. A local doctor was brought in to give whatever care was available, but really all we could do was wait and pray. My father was always extremely conscientious about his work, but he would leave his office every few hours to sit at my brother's bedside.

"Pray for your brother, Ashraf," my mother said, as she brought me the Koran. I couldn't read the words, but I put the Holy Book on my head and sat up till dawn, praying and hoping, not daring to imagine a life without my brother. During the weeks he lay ill, I could almost feel his fever and experience his symptoms. Even in later years the bond between us would affect me most in times of trouble. When he was ill, it was almost as if I were ill; when he was hurt, I would share his pain. My brother did recover, of course, though the illness left him with an enlarged spleen, as sometimes is the case with typhoid. As soon as he was strong enough to stand on his feet, it was work as usual.

My father was acutely aware of his own lack of formal education, and he was determined that we should have one, including at least a foreign language. He hired Madame Arfa, the French wife of a Persian army officer, to teach us French, but the time we spent with her wasn't like work at all, because she opened up a new and unknown world to us, a magical foreign world that revolved around a city called Paris.

"Paris is called the 'City of Light,'" she would say, "because the streets are never dark, not even at night. These streets are paved, and they're safe enough for people to enjoy at any hour of the day. Paris is filled with beautiful shops, with theaters and opera houses, with fine restaurants and cinemas."

I couldn't help comparing Paris and Teheran. Persia's capital city was not a very inspiring sight in those days. We had our traditional oriental bazaars, which looked exactly as they must have centuries ago; a few shops which stocked

16

imported goods; a few segregated cinemas, where women sat in one section, the men in another, watching old American movies while a translator explained to the audience what was going on; and the Muslim theater, which was devoted to dramatizing the life and death of the martyrs of our religion. This was the sum total of our cultural life, as well as our "tourist attractions."

Many of the houses were hovels made of mud or brick. The streets, which were unpaved and unappealing even in daylight, were taken over by bands of wandering bandits and cutthroats after dark. It was hard to imagine people strolling through Teheran enjoying themselves. They were more likely to be found in the teahouses and opium dens, where they tried, for a little while, to forget the miserable condition of their lives.

It is no wonder I could never get enough of Madame Arfa's stories, and she found in me a very attentive pupil, one who would gladly stay after school and ask for more.

"My dear Princess," she would continue, "I'm sure that someday you'll go to Paris and see for yourself—the buildings that have several stories with machines called elevators that take you to the top. All the houses have clean drinking water, and most people can read and write. Men and women work together, in offices and factories, and at night they go out, to dine together and dance. And no one wears a veil."

I found these descriptions as incredible as anything I had heard in my bedtime fairy tales. Clean drinking water was not something anyone took for granted in Teheran, even among the royal family. Men and women lived segregated lives, coming together only in the framework of the family and only in the privacy of their own homes. I had rarely seen an adult woman without a veil; my own mother kept her face covered in the presence of men.

I knew, and Madame Arfa's stories served to make it clearer, that I didn't want this life of a typical Persian housewife, even one who was well off. To me it seemed a very limited life, circumscribed by the nursery and the kitchen walls, by days filled with the company of other women, drinking tea and gossiping. My thoughts turned in another direction, and I applied myself diligently to my lessons, especially my French.

Once a week I had a day off from school to go with my nanny to the *hammam*, the communal bath that was a traditional part of the old-style villas and palaces. I suppose the *hammam* was Persia's version of the health spa, since it allowed girls and women to sit around the round marble tubs, soaking up the steam from the hot water, talking and laughing as they washed their hair and scrubbed themselves with the *leefas*. Since this was a social as well as a hygienic interlude, the day would include lunch and maybe even a nap inside the *hammam*. My father gave me an allowance of 100 *toman* ($15) a month, so I could finish off my weekly outing by sending a boy into town to buy some sweets for dessert.

Yet I much preferred the weekend—Thursday and Friday in Muslim countries—when I would join my brother and his friends. All of us were enthusiastic riders, and some days I might spend as many as five or six hours on horseback. Whenever we raced our horses, I came in first more often than not, which led me to question the tenacious myth of male supremacy.

Cars, especially American ones, were another passion we all shared. When I was still very young, Father bought me my first car, a yellow Ford convertible, vintage 1930, as I recall. As soon as I could reach all the controls and master them, I was allowed to drive the car around the palace grounds. I loved that car and the feeling of freedom and power it gave me.

In spite of all these "male" activities, I never really wished I was a boy. I liked the idea of being female, though I never accepted the structured roles that were imposed on women. The male role, with all its options and prerogatives, .

seemed infinitely more interesting, and perhaps that is why I've lived most of my life working in the world of men.

With no girlfriends my own age, I adopted by brother's friends as my own. I was often thrown together with a kind and very gentle boy called Mehrpur. His father, Teymourtash, was my father's Minister of Court, and so we had numerous opportunities to be together. We rode and played tennis and talked, and soon the matchmakers started to see a possible future marriage for us. I was still a child, with no thought at all of love and marriage, but in those days it wasn't at all uncommon to betroth children at a very tender age, even from the womb, providing they turned out to be the right sex.

This prospective match never got very far because Mehrpur's father was accused of complicity in a political plot against my father. He was jailed, and the rest of the family (except for Mehrpur, who spent a year at school in Switzerland) was sent back to the village they had come from. Mehrpur and I met shortly before he left. We talked about seeing each other again in the future, though we knew this reunion might be a long way off. Since I didn't make friends very easily, I felt the loss of Mehrpur's company, though my brother tried to console me.

This loss, however, was nothing compared to the grief I felt when my father also announced at the same time that the Crown Prince would be sent abroad to continue his studies at Le Rosey, the exclusive school in Switzerland. He would be accompanied by my brother Ali Reza, Mehrpur, the Crown Prince's friend Hussein Fardust (a man who ironically played a tragic role in our lives in recent years), and my half-brothers. But I would be left behind.

Now I would really come to know what loneliness was. After my brother left, I felt as if I had been separated from a part of myself, and I spent the next few months just going through the motions of living, not really caring about anything I did.

In time, this separation led me to realize that although my brother and I were like faces in a mirror, I needed a life of my own if I was to survive—an identity separate from that of my twin. I thought perhaps an education, some sort of work, might be the answer, so I attacked my lessons with even more than my usual intensity.

Throwing myself into those lessons I found a new love—mathematics. The precision and exactness of this discipline suited me, and with my teacher's encouragement I moved very quickly to higher and higher levels. I invested in my studies all the time and energy I had once given to sports with my brother, establishing the pattern that would stay with me for a lifetime: to this day, I have no hobbies. My interest is in my work. My father, too, reinforced this pattern; although an education abroad was out of the question for a woman, he was pleased whenever I moved to a more advanced level, and he would reward me with one of his rare moments of praise and perhaps the gift of a jewel.

Perhaps my father knew how miserable I was, because after my brother had been gone for two years, he announced that Mother, my sister, and I were going to Switzerland to visit the Crown Prince. From the moment I heard the news until the time we left Teheran, my behavior was impeccable, lest my father find a reason to change his mind. I couldn't really believe that I was going to see my brother and Madame Arfa's marvelous Europe at the same time.

Traveling from Iran to Europe was not a simple matter in those days. We went by car from Teheran to Bandar Pahlavi, a port on the southern coast of the Caspian Sea. There we boarded a Russian ship, which took us to Baku, on the Soviet shores of the Sea. I couldn't sleep at all during the sea voyage. I lay awake, restless with anticipation, trying to imagine the adventures ahead. The rest of our journey—through the Soviet Union, Poland, and Germany—was made by train.

Each time we stopped at a station, I was amazed at the

number of people milling around. The structured and sheltered life of the palace hadn't prepared me for what I was seeing: the rapidly changing landscapes, the exotic-looking people, the fast pace of the European cities through which we traveled. I studied them all, wanting to implant every detail in my memory.

Although I wasn't supposed to leave the train when it stopped, I stole off whenever I had the chance. Everything excited me, even the simple sight of people greeting newly arrived passengers or seeing friends off. Here was the reality that matched Madame Arfa's stories. Women were indeed walking, unveiled, with men.

Always there were the vendors, selling an intoxicating variety of wares: clothing and sunflower seeds and dilled cucumbers. I tried to buy some of the things I saw, but I couldn't speak any of the languages I heard.

Each time I was absent from the train, I would hold my breath, even while I savored the details of secret explorations. I was accustomed to doing what I was told, even when I didn't like it, so I was always relieved when I got back to the train without being found out.

Our train journey lasted for eight days, not including a two-day stopover in Berlin, the first major European city I saw. The year was 1933, and my mother and I were met by the German government's Chief of Protocol and escorted to the Iranian Embassy, where we found a large bouquet of flowers from Chancellor Adolf Hitler. None of us had any idea then what forces he would unleash on the world, and what this would mean to Iran. That night I saw my first operetta—I think it was *The Merry Widow*—and although the music was foreign to my ears, the splendor of the opera house and the glitter of the audience were enough to hold my attention throughout the evening.

After we boarded the train once more, my impatience to reach Switzerland, to see my brother again, made me so excited I could hardly stay in my seat. When we arrived, I

21

practically jumped off the train before it came to a full stop.

I fell in love with Switzerland at once, with the breathtakingly beautiful landscape that seemed to be reflected in the healthy, happy appearance of the people.

My brother looked healthy and happy, too, stronger and more fit than he had been in Teheran. I saw at once how much he had been influenced by Europe and by Western customs. Before he left Teheran, he had been, in spite of his quiet nature, a little rough around the edges. In moments of excitement he might swing from a tree or ride his horse into the house, but now his manners had been refined and Europeanized.

We had two years' worth of catching up to do, so we spent long hours talking together; within a very short time it was as if we hadn't been apart at all. I've had this experience with my brother many times since. No matter how many miles separate us, or how many months or years, the minute we see each other again, there is no distance between us at all.

My brother told me how impressed he had been by the democratic attitudes he had seen at school, by the fact that all the boys, whether they were sons of businessmen or noblemen or kings, were equals within the school community. He talked about how he had come to realize for the first time how much economic and social disparity there was among the people of Iran.

In the two years since I had last seen him my brother had also become an accomplished athlete, the versatile sportsman he would be in the years to come. He was especially proud of being chosen captain of the soccer team, and he also told me about two new friends he had made, diverse as they were. One of these was Richard Helms, who later became director of the Central Intelligence Agency and America's Ambassador to Iran. Another was Ernest Perron, the son of the school handyman, a young man who came to live in Iran and remained my brother's close friend until the day he died in 1961.

Seeing my brother again, seeing what life was like in Switzerland, made me desperately want to stay. I knew that it would be difficult to get my father's permission, and I was too afraid to ask when he telephoned Le Rosey from Turkey. (He had gone to see the man who had inspired so many of his plans for Iran, Mustafa Kemal, and he took advantage of the international phone system, which we didn't have in Iran.) I sent a telegram, asking if I might remain and study in a European school.

His answer was a short, harsh cable: "Stop this nonsense and come home at once." There was no explanation; but this too was typical of Reza Shah. I was furious and disappointed and hurt when I realized that no matter how much education my father might allow at home, I would always be denied the opportunities he gave my brothers. Disappointed and angry though I was, I didn't dream of disobeying. In the Middle Eastern world, fathers were obeyed even when they weren't kings.

My father's answer closed the door forever on a dream that had become for a little while more real and more compelling than the life that was charted for me. For a brief, tantalizing moment I had seen the reality of a world where a woman could develop her capabilities, could shape and form her own life. In Europe I had seen it, touched it, experienced it, but now the moment was over for me. I vowed that in the years to come I would find a way to make contact with Europe and the Western world.

There would be other disappointments ahead, doors that would open a crack, showing me a glimpse of something exciting, something true and valuable and worth reaching for, and then they would close. But that first disappointment, the university education I was denied, has stayed with me. I've learned a great deal from life, from travel, books, and experience, but every so often, especially in the company of intelligent, articulate people, I feel a certain inadequacy, a sense of something undeveloped and untried in me.

The thought of leaving Europe and returning to my disciplined, lonely life in Teheran was extremely painful. When I returned home, I felt the same sense of loss I had experienced when my brother first went to Switzerland. There would be two more lonely years for me, and it must have been at that time that the seeds of my future international career were planted, a career that no doubt was in part motivated by the need to make up for that first frustration.

Ironically, it was during the years following my visit to Le Rosey, a time when I was most unhappy, that my father took a major step in changing the lives of Persian women.

Reza Shah was determined to "Westernize" Persia, to bring it into the twentieth century, since it was in the West that he saw the most dynamic expressions of prosperity and power. To do this, to make us prosperous and powerful, he could not afford to leave our women, half of Persia's small population, inactive and covered. He decided to abolish the *chador*, the traditional veil. Here again was an example of the paradox that was my father. Though I never felt he was willing to relax his strict control over us at home, he did make the historic decision to present the Queen, my sister Shams, and me, unveiled, to the population of Teheran. To Reza Shah, as to any Persian man, anything concerning his wife and family was a private matter. You could sooner ask him how much money he earned or how much his house cost before you could ask personal questions about his wife or daughters. At home my father was very much a man of an earlier generation (I remember he ordered me to change my clothes "at once" because I had appeared at lunch in a sleeveless dress). But as the king, he was prepared to put aside his strong personal feelings in the interest of bringing progress to his country.

When he had made his decision, he came to us and said, "This is the hardest thing I've ever had to do, but I must ask you to serve as an example for other Persian women." My mother, my sister Shams, and I were to take part in a ceremony at the new Teheran Teacher's College and we were to do so unveiled. In the winter of 1934 the people saw, for the first time, what the Queen and her daughters looked like.

After this ceremony, all women were required to remove their veils, and those who refused were forced to do so. My father knew that he could build schools and create employment opportunities for women, but he also knew that these measures would be useless unless women were pushed out of their cloistered environment. Women were going to enter the mainstream of society—*de gré ou de force.*

After our public appearance, my father had our photographs published in the newspapers. When one mullah publicly condemned the Shah for allowing the women of his family to show their faces, one of my father's generals responded with an equally public gesture: he pulled the turban (the symbol of his religious office) from the clergyman's head and then shaved his beard. My father was always a deeply religious man, but he realized that many of the practices and customs that contributed to Persia's backward condition were relics of social traditions and not fundamental to the religion of Islam.

Naturally, there was continued resistance to the Shah's edict concerning the veil, and to the emancipation of women in general. The mullahs saw it, quite correctly, as a threat to their authority and to the body of ancient tradition of which they had made themselves the guardians. There is an important distinction here between what is written in the Koran and the *interpretation* of it by individual mullahs. It is a distinction that must be made if we are to make any sense of the excesses committed at this moment in the name of

25

"Islam." Actually, it was the intent of our religion to *protect* women from the harshness of pre-Islamic Arabian customs; it was not the intention to repress them for centuries. Islam ended the Arabian practice of killing unwanted female babies. It also limited the number of wives a man might have to four, in a society where men had been taking as many wives as they wished. The rule of inheritance, whereby a woman inherits only half as much as her brothers, was historically not as discriminatory as it now seems, but rather a recognition of the fact that after her father died, a woman's brothers were responsible for her, financially and socially.

Even the veil was not required by the Koran. The Koran instructed women to be modest in their dress and demeanor; this precept led to the veil, a relic in the modern world, now revived in Muslim countries more as an anti-Western political symbol than as a return to religious mandate.

In the Persia of that day a woman was said to have "more hair than brains," and she was treated accordingly. Legally and socially she was a ward of her father, her brother, or her husband. Under the civil code she could not hold public office or even pursue a higher education. In court, her testimony counted half as much as that of a man. A husband was absolute head of the family. He could forbid his wife to travel, to hold a job, or even to have a bank account. He had the right to as many as four wives and as many concubines as he could afford. He could divorce any wife at will (for a woman, divorce was extremely difficult) and take custody of his children as soon as they were weaned.

Obviously the men of Persia, the decision makers, were not going to give up such absolute power without serious resistance. Nor were the women, for that matter, ready to exchange the protection they had traditionally enjoyed for the unknowns of a new social status.

It is equally obvious, and certainly it became painfully clear in the years following my father's regime, that no ruler can legislate a social revolution. He can implement the outward form of social change, but he cannot legislate change in the minds of the people. Stable and lasting social change has to evolve slowly and gradually, over a period of many generations. When my brother became king, he became aware of this reality, and he even allowed the use of the veil by those who clung to it (the Communists made similar concessions to Christianity, particularly in their satellite countries). But at the time Reza Shah was king, no such concessions seemed possible, for if Persia was to survive in a world of technology and rapid change, it could no longer afford the consequences of living in the past.

My brother finished his studies in Switzerland in 1936 and sent word that he was coming home at last. It was one of the happiest days of my life. The entire family went to meet him at Bandar Pahlavi, the port he had departed from four years before. I was surprised at how much the town had changed since I had last seen it. Now there was a broad modern boulevard, with electric lights lining the shoreline. It wasn't as grand as a European port, but it was a visible sign of my father's modernization programs.

My brother was no longer a schoolboy; he was even more dignified and mature than when I had last seen him at Le Rosey. I watched as ministers, members of Parliament, and other high officials came to greet him. To me he was still the brother of my childhood, but it was clear that in the eyes of Iran he was the future king.

To complete his training for the throne, my brother was then enrolled in Teheran Military College. Although I didn't know it, plans were also being made for me, plans that would bring my childhood, like his, to an end and throw me abruptly into exactly the kind of adult life I had tried desperately to escape.

# · III ·

# WEDDINGS

There were rumors in the palace that my father had found husbands for Shams and me. My nanny, my servants, and even my mother started congratulating me, but to my 17-year-old mind this was dreaded news. I shrank from the idea of marriage, let alone marriage to a man I had never seen. I was afraid to express my feelings to my father, so I asked my brother to intercede, to ask Reza Shah to change his mind.

My brother listened sympathetically, but when I had finished, he held out little hope. "Trying to change our father's mind on this matter would be a waste of time," he said. "He believes a girl should marry at a certain age, and opposing him is useless. I think you must do as he says."

The first time I caught a glimpse of the two prospective bridegrooms, they were playing tennis with my brother. My future husband was to be Fereydoun Jam, a young army officer and son of the Prime Minister, and my sister was to marry a man called Ali Qavam, a member of a prominent Shiraz family. Naturally, I took notice only of the man chosen for me. I must admit that I found him tall, handsome, and rather elegant, although I still wasn't enthusiastic about the idea of marriage. Unfortunately, Shams decided she was more attracted to my fiancé than she was to the man our father had chosen for her. As the elder sister, she had certain prerogatives, so the fiancés were officially exchanged.

I took an instant dislike to Ali Qavam. Whether it was because I didn't find him as attractive as Fereydoun Jam, or whether it was because he was being forced on me, I don't know. I sat in my room and cried for a week.

"You mustn't act like this," my mother said, trying to comfort me. "Your fiancé is a good man, educated in England, and he comes from a very good family." But I refused to be consoled, knowing that my only choices were either to marry or to be disowned. I knew that my father would never tolerate an act of defiance by any of his children.

So I was married, in a traditional double ceremony with Shams, complete with white Lanvin wedding dress, though black would have been more suitable to my mood.

The only thing that pleased me about my marriage was the adult status that came with it. As a married woman I was allowed to drive my car every day to my new sister-in-law's house, a distance of about 20 kilometers. There I could enjoy a long workout on the tennis court, followed by tea and pastry and a diverting visit with my new relatives. To a happily married woman these visits might have seemed dull and routine, but for me, the time I spent in my car, playing tennis, or talking to my in-laws, was a way of avoiding the realities of my marriage.

Throughout my marriage I avoided Ali Qavam whenever it was humanly possible. Perhaps I would have reacted in the same way to anyone who was forced on me as he was, but I never saw him as anything but a cold, calculating, and most unattractive man, eminently unlikeable and certainly unlovable.

30

My husband seemed oddly untroubled by my lack of enthusiasm or by the fact that there was no love lost between us. He seemed satisifed to be the nominal husband of a princess, and not particularly concerned about whether or not we had any meaningful life together. We never discussed our feelings, but from the beginning of our marriage we slept in separate bedrooms and lived separate lives.

Although I had my own house on Kakh Avenue, a spacious, modern, Western-style villa, I left there late each morning, drove to the palace, and had lunch with my brother. After lunch, I stayed several more hours, postponing my return home as long as I could. At the palace I could retreat into more familiar patterns and on the occasional afternoons when my brother did not have to attend to his official duties, we rode, played tennis, or bridge, one of his favorite games. As long as I was with him, I didn't have to think about my miserable marriage. The thought of divorce crossed my mind more than once, but there was no one I dared discuss it with. Even if I thought my father might be sympathetic (I didn't for a minute have that hope), I knew he was intensely preoccupied with affairs of state.

The task he had set for himself was monumental, to say the least, for he meant, by the sheer force of his will and determination, to take Iran from the Middle Ages to the Modern Age—an evolutionary process that had taken centuries in Western Europe. High on Reza Shah's agenda for the change was the development of a strong central government, and to this end he spent an entire decade pacifying the major tribes—the Bakhtiari, the Qashqai, the Kurds, the Lurs—and bringing them under his authority. Without a well-developed infrastructure of roads and communications (this too was a major priority of his regime), this pacification came only after scores of military expeditions by the king's troops into some of Iran's harshest and most inaccessible terrain.

Although these campaigns were carried out on horseback and on foot, with mules as weapons carriers, my father knew that the days of the foot soldier and the simple cavalryman were numbered. He saw the need for a modern, unified, and decently paid army (during his own military career a soldier might have to find supplementary work in order to feed his family). He reorganized—or rather created—the first formal Iranian military establishment, with standardized training and a machinery for conscription. He built factories to produce modern rifles and other small arms (some of his army's weapons had been virtual museum pieces), and he infused his troops with a sense of pride and status that Persia's armies had not known since the eighteenth century.

Against the influence of the mullahs, he waged a different kind of campaign than that against the tribes. Before my father's reign, judicial powers were held by the clergy. As part of his plan to turn Persia into a modern Iran, he introduced a Western-style (predominantly French) judicial system, which included a hierarchy of courts, as well as civil, commercial, and criminal codes. These new measures to separate mosque and state, later expanded by my brother, led to powerful forces of reaction against the monarchy; this opposition would come to a head decades later. For although the mullahs were traditional supporters of the king, they would, when deprived of their powers (and later, during land reforms, of their wealth), turn against the throne and establish their own alliances elsewhere.

Realizing that the influence of the mullahs depended in large part on the ignorance of the masses, and knowing that a modern nation could not be built by a nation of illiterates, Reza Shah instituted a plan of compulsory primary education and built hundreds of schools, including the University of Teheran, completed in 1934. He began the practice, which continued under my brother, of giving government scholarships to qualified Iranian students who wished to study abroad. Ironically, this practice, too, would create a crucial focal point of anti-Pahlavi sentiment in the years to come.

It would be impossible here to give a full account of the sweeping changes my father made in Iran; perhaps only a study of "before" and "after" photographs would show just how dramatic a transformation there was in so short a time. Reza Shah built roads, hospitals, and ports where none had existed; he standardized the antiquated system of monetary units, weights, and measures, and instituted a relatively modern banking system. One of his proudest achievements was the building of the Trans-Iranian Railway, which took 12 years to complete and which today is still considered a marvel of modern engineering. Even this railway would come to have negative political implications in the years to come.

In short, Reza Shah would enjoy a sense of accomplishment known to few rulers in the modern world. He had been born in a country that traveled by horse and by mule, yet he lived to see that country's first air links to several foreign countries. He had grown up in a nation of farmers and herders, yet he lived to see the establishment of Persian industry: factories that produced textiles, food products, footwear, building materials, chemicals, and munitions.

Of course, he knew that his was only a beginning, but in those early days he was confident that he could make all his plans and programs a reality, whatever the opposition. This opposition came not only from those who were losers in his reforms, such as the clergy, but also from those who were beneficiaries. (In later years my brother would experience a similar twin-pronged opposition: criticism from conservative elements who said he did "too much, too soon" and criticism from Western observers and the Iranian left, who said he did "too little, too late.") For example, on one of his visits to a remote village, Reza Shah saw many villagers living in very primitive shacks, sharing these quarters with their livestock. Almost immediately he built for these people a "model village" of simple but functional modern houses. Reluctantly the villagers moved into these houses, only because the king said they should. But in later years, after the end of Reza Shah's reign, they abandoned the houses and moved back into their shacks, livestock and all. Although I am an Iranian and understand more about our tradition than Westerners do, I am at a loss to explain this kind of stubborn resistance to change.

With his eye so much on the future, my father could not neglect the vital issue of the royal succession. His daughters safely married, he now turned his attention to finding a suitable wife for the Crown Prince. The ideal candidate would have to be a royal princess, preferably one who could bring Iran closer to another country. My father made a series of inquiries throughout the Middle East, and after several preliminary talks between the courts of Teheran and Cairo, it was announced in 1938 that Crown Prince Mohammed Reza Pahlavi would marry Princess Fawzia, sister of Egypt's King Farouk.

As soon as the arrangements had been made, my father asked the Parliament to declare Fawzia an Iranian (so that her children would also be Iranians). He rushed the construction work on the Marble Palace, which he had started building several years before, so it might be finished in time for the wedding celebration. Reza Shah loved to build, and his Marble Palace, though far less ornamental than the Golestan Palace, reflected his pleasure in Iran's local crafts. Surrounded by a sprawling park-like garden of roses, mimosa, weeping willows, cypress, and pine, the Marble Palace (actually the word "palace" is something of a misnomer for this very lovely house of only 12 rooms) was distinguished by its walls of light-green Persian marble and by two especially beautiful rooms: my father's office, decorated with mosaic patterns of inlaid wood, and the ballroom of mirrorwork, with its typically Iranian dome.

This palace would be the scene for the "second celebration" of my brother's wedding. The first was in Cairo, and since our family did not attend, I eagerly studied the newspaper photographs of my new sister-in-law. I had heard that this dark-haired Egyptian Princess with creamy skin and expressive blue-gray eyes was quite beautiful, and I wondered if she would make my brother happy.

During the years that my brother was married to Fawzia, and in the course of his two later marriages, there would be endless gossip printed about my rivalry with one sister-in-law or another. But the simple truth that has dictated my relationships with all of my sisters-in-law is considerably less colorful: I have always tried to love anyone who is an important part of my brother's life because, for me, that is part of loving him.

In fact with Fawzia I had an instant rapport. I can still remember the day my mother, my sister, and I went to the port of Khorramshahr in southern Iran to greet the newlyweds arriving from Egypt. Both my brother and his wife were radiant, and when they looked at each other, it was with eyes full of affection. Like my own marriage, theirs had been an arranged match; but unlike mine, theirs was a union in which bride and groom actually liked each other.

Princess Fawzia became the first really close woman friend I had. Like my brother's two later wives, she was fairly reserved, even a little cool at times, but kindhearted and generous. I knew she would miss her family and the life she had enjoyed in Egypt, so I tried my best to make her feel comfortable. Though I had never visited Egypt, I knew that the court life of Cairo (which was then known as the "Paris of the Middle East") was far livelier and more glittering than anything we had to offer in Teheran. Of course we had come

35

a long way since my childhood, when the most exciting social events of the year were the "mourning teas" during the month of Muharram, at which the mullah would proceed to tell in vivid detail how the martyrs of our religion met their deaths.

My father had tried to discourage these and other ritual forms of mourning, such as self-flagellation, that are characteristic of our religion, in favor of more joyous and secular holidays (such as the Persian New Year) marked by feasting, picnicking, or some form of pageantry. But still we were a long way from Cairo, which had an opera as well as theater, cinema, and dance. Teheran's cultural life was limited to Muslim theater and a few movie houses.

Still Fawzia and I had some pleasant times together. The Pahlavis had an active family life, and we would watch movies at home (this was one of our royal luxuries), listen to music—Persian, or Egyptian in honor of Fawzia—play cards, or just visit with one another. Occasionally Fawzia and I would go into the city for lunch and perhaps some window-shopping at one of the few stores that carried a rich variety of imported goods not found in our local bazaars.

As the wife of the Crown Prince, Fawzia was expected to have a child, preferably a son, as soon as possible. One day she came to me with a rather whimsical proposal. How would I feel, she asked, about the idea of trying to become pregnant at the same time, so we could share the months of waiting together? Now considering the fact that I couldn't abide my husband, it may seem strange that I even considered this idea. But consider it I did. Though I was an "old married woman," I was still a teenager, and this girlish conspiracy, with the prospect of a baby to fill the gaps in my life, appealed to me. In truth I was so sexually naive and so repelled by my husband that I had to take what we would now call a tranquilizer before I could bring myself to share his bed.

Naturally our scheme didn't work: we became pregnant at different times. I conceived first, and when I gave birth to my son Shahram, Fawzia—only three months pregnant—was there to congratulate me. Her daughter Shahnaz was born six months later. After the visit from Fawzia, my father and my brother arrived to offer their good wishes and congratulations. Only my husband did not come to see his child that day—which leaves little doubt about the state of our relationship then.

This distance between us grew even worse after Shahram was born. There was so much alienation that I could not even bear to be in the same room with him. I broached the idea of divorce to my brother. He was sympathetic, but he thought our father would never allow a royal family divorce. He told me to be patient.

And although I didn't know it when we talked, the world was soon to be plunged into such crisis that all of my own personal problems would quickly become inconsequential.

# THE WAR YEARS

One morning, as I was brushing my hair in my bedroom, I heard someone call my name from the garden. I opened the window and saw my brother.

"Germany has invaded Poland" he said.

It was September 3, 1939, and the world war that we had dreaded and had speculated so much about had become a reality. I knew that we were extremely vulnerable given our "crossroads" position between Europe and Asia. At home, the main topic of discussion was the threat of war. My father knew that if we were dragged into the conflict as we had been in World War I, all of his development plans for Iran would have to be abandoned. History proved that he had been more than right.

Shortly after the attack on Poland, Iran proclaimed its neutrality. Although my father did not like Hitler and never supported him, I must admit he did derive some satisfaction from seeing the German challenge to Britain and Russia, Iran's long-standing enemies. Our hopes for neutrality, however, would last only until the summer of 1941, when

Germany marched on Russia. Now the Allies had to find a way to get supplies into the U.S.S.R. They had no choice but to use either Turkey or Iran as an overland "bridge," and they decided on Iran, which offered strategic advantages.

To cross the borders of a neutral country, the Allies needed some pretext. They could have asked my father for his cooperation in creating a supply route to Russia, but instead they accused us of being Nazi sympathizers because of the presence of German engineers, industrialists, and other technical experts who had come to work on various development programs. They "suggested" that Reza Shah expel these German nationals from Iran, perhaps knowing full well that he would be reluctant to do so. Such a move would not only deprive Iran of valuable technical assistance; but more crucial, it might antagonize the Hitler government, which would see such an expulsion of civilian personnel as a violation of our professed neutrality. The continued presence of these Germans gave Anthony Eden and Vyacheslav Molotov just the excuse they needed to enter Iran from both the northern and southern borders and to establish the supply routes to Russia.

And so on August 25, 1941, the day we had feared (it still stands out in my mind) arrived and, with it, the sequence of events that would end the reign of Reza Shah and bring years of hardship to Iran. My father came to lunch looking so tense and so grim that none of us dared to speak. "What I knew was inevitable has happened," he said. "The Allies have invaded. I think this will be the end for me—the English will see to it." He felt especially apprehensive because his Prime Minister, Ali Mansour, had neglected to inform him that such an invasion was imminent. Apparently Iran's diplomatic representatives in Europe had cabled the Prime Minister that an Allied attack was almost certain, but this information had not been passed on to my father. Reza Shah felt that such an omission meant that those who opposed him in his own government probably had made a secret agreement with the Allies.

My brother was concerned not only about the consequences of war, but also about the threat to the monarchy, the gravest threat to Reza Shah's reign since the time of his coronation. He doubted that the Iranian army would be able to hold the palace in the event of an Allied attack. Later that afternoon he brought me a gun and said: "Ashraf, keep this gun with you, and if troops enter Teheran and try to take us, fire a few shots and then take your own life. I'll do the same." I took the gun and promised to do as he asked.

On the second day of the invasion, Allied airplanes carried out a light bombing over Teheran. Frightened by the sound of bombs and anti-aircraft guns, I held my little son tightly in my arms and started for the basement. My husband stopped me. "Give me the boy," he said. "I'm going to take him to the British Embassy." (His family had close ties with the British.)

"Never," I answered. "This is my son, and he stays with me." We fought bitterly over the child, but I wouldn't budge.

That same night my father decided to evacuate all of us to the city of Isfahan (350 kilometers south of Teheran), which he felt would be relatively safe because it was far from any frontier. Although Isfahan is one of the world's loveliest cities, with its spacious boulevards and squares, regal palaces and azure blue mosques, during that visit we spent most of our days around the radio, trying to get some news of what was happening.

We heard that my father had removed Ali Mansour and appointed a new prime minister, Mohammed Ali Foroughi, who had quickly arranged peace terms with the Allies. This was more of a formality than anything else, since Iran's army had been immobilized within days and its small navy sunk. Yet the Allies still did not trust Reza Shah, since he was clearly not the kind of ruler who would cooperate with the governments of countries that had invaded Iran. There followed a campaign against him over the airwaves. The BBC, the British-controlled Radio Delhi, and Radio Moscow attacked the Shah, telling the Iranians they had a dictator for a king and calling for his resignation. Radio Berlin urged the Shah to resist. On September 16, 1941—22 days after the invasion—my father realized that in order to save the throne, he had no choice but to abdicate. Radio Teheran announced that the new Shah was Mohammed Reza Pahlavi.

The next day, as I was sitting at the window of the house in Isfahan looking down into the courtyard, I saw a very old man walking with two companions. As they drew closer, I was stunned to realize that this "old man" in civilian clothes was my father. In less than a month he seemed to have aged twenty years. Looking back, I think it is possible that he may have suffered some kind of stroke immediately following his abdication.

In my whole life I had never seen Reza Shah in anything but a military uniform, and I had never known him to be anything other than a proud and vigorous man. His work had been the activating force of his life, and now he was suddenly a man without purpose, sent to join the realm of old men whose usefulness has ended. At my brother's wedding he had expressed the wish to have ten more years to finish the programs he had started, but he was not to have that wish.

My father shared our vigil at the radio and our anxiety as to whether my brother could keep the country together under the disruption of foreign occupation. The Shah's first task would be the painful one of cooperating with the armies of occupation while at the same time trying to maintain whatever he could of our country's integrity. I was confident that he had the capability of doing the job that would be expected of him; his Western education and his ease with Westerners would serve him well, I thought. Yet I worried about the enormous pressures he faced.

The day the new Shah, 22-year-old Mohammed Reza Pahlavi, went to take the oath of office, we listened to the radio, hearing the shouts of "Long live the Shah" when the royal carriage passed. Yet we knew he would need much more than the acclaim of the crowds to see him through the critical times ahead. Later it was announced that Parliament had given the Shah a thunderous ovation, with the diplomats of all the foreign powers present, except those of Britain and Russia.

Although my father had been removed from the throne, the Allies were still not satisfied; they still feared Reza Shah, and they decided to quickly send him into exile. My father asked if he might be allowed to go to Argentina and the Allies agreed. On a bright, sunny autumn day in 1941, my father and the other members of our family, with the exception of Fawzia, Shahnaz, my son Shahram, and me, were taken by car out of Isfahan to a ship in the Persian Gulf, 600 kilometers away. The Shah boarded the English ship still under the impression that he was going to Argentina, and it was not until the vessel was out to sea that he discovered the British had changed their minds and decided to send him elsewhere. His exile began on the island of Mauritius and ended in Johannesburg, South Africa.

During my father's last days in Isfahan I had repeatedly asked him to take me with him. Each time he answered: "I would love to have you with me, but your brother needs you more. I want you to stay with him." Then he would add: "I wish you had been a boy, so you could be a brother to him now."

For my father, those last few days were solitary, quiet ones, and at night we would talk or I would read to him. He seemed less intimidating now, more approachable than I had ever known him to be. One evening I gathered up my courage and started to tell him how unhappy I was in my marriage and how much I wanted a divorce. I don't know exactly what kind of reaction I had expected, but I wasn't prepared for the sad smile and the pat on the shoulder he gave me. "But *babi*," he said, using the Persian endearment of childhood, "why didn't you tell me how unhappy you were? Why didn't you tell me sooner?"

"I didn't dare," I answered. "I was afraid to anger you."

He smiled again and took my hand. "I don't want you to worry about this marriage any longer. As soon as I can, I will write to your brother and tell him to help you with a divorce." The actual divorce would in fact take almost a year, since my husband was not eager to relinquish the social position he had enjoyed.

After my father left us, Fawzia and I started back to the capital. My brother came to the holy city of Shahrary, 10 kilometers south of Teheran, to welcome us back. (In Iran it's customary, when you are expecting honored guests or loved ones back from a journey, to travel forward part of the distance to greet them.) Our sadness over my father's exile lifted a little when we caught our first glimpse of Mohammed Reza Pahlavi as the new Shah of Iran.

The end of Reza Shah's strong reign had set the stage for continued foreign intervention and domestic political intrigues. At 22, my brother could not have the power my father had had, so what followed was a variation of the scenario that had played itself out in the years of the Qajar dynasty before my father came to power, the pattern that repeated itself whenever there was an absence of a strong and cohesive central government.

Yet what was a difficult period for the monarchy was even harsher for the average Iranian citizen, who faced scarcity and up to 400 percent inflation during the war years. The Iranian became a second-class citizen in his own country, living in the shadow of foreign troops, ignored or pushed aside to satisfy the needs of foreign powers.

How could we ignore the lesson of these years when we saw that in spite of all the Western talk about "self-determination," there was always the naked reality that stronger nations could impose their will on weaker ones? How could we not feel bitter toward the nations that occupied us when the transit roads all the way from the Persian Gulf to the Russian borders, as well as the railroad, were under Allied control? Every means of transportation was used, 24 hours a day, to move food, drugs, and military supplies to Russia. Though they hadn't fought a war or lost one, Iranians were treated like the citizens of a defeated country. If they wanted to travel anywhere within their own country, they had to obtain special visas from the Allied military government. The people could not use their own roads but were expected instead to wait on the shoulders with their mules or wagons or cars, sometimes for hours at a time, until the military supply caravans passed. Since many of our roads were still unpaved, great clouds of dust were raised by the lines of vehicles, and when their waiting was over, the people would be covered with a thick layer of dust, as if they had passed through a desert sandstorm.

At the ports and railway stations, war supplies were given top priority while Iranian cargoes had to wait for weeks or months. If an artist were to paint a typical landscape of the war period, it would have to include long gray lines of foreign Studebaker trucks winding their way along the rugged country roads, past the inevitable clusters of peasants waiting patiently with their horses and mules.

In the city there were long lines, too, in front of bakeries and grocery shops. While the Russians diverted the rice and wheat of northern provinces for their own use, Teheran was filled with posters telling the people that the Allies were importing wheat from Canada to feed *them* and that Allied troops were fighting for *their* freedom. The ranks of hungry, miserable people were increased by the tens of thousands of Poles who had fled their own country and now spilled over the Russian border into Iran.

There was one area in which we had no shortages:

45

when the American troops came to Iran, they had money to spend during their off-duty hours, and bars and nightclubs sprang up all over the capital, to accommodate the affluent GI. Hungry women took to the streets to earn enough money to eat. This type of Western influence in a Muslim country fueled the indignation of the mullahs.

The foreign armies that occupied Iran—the Russians, the British, and now the Americans—were called the "Allies," but each of their governments was actively engaged in the familiar practice of serving its own interests, each one trying to gain a strong foothold in Iran for itself. A shrewd observer could have seen in Iran the seeds of the future cold war.

The divided Allies also divided Iranians into several factions or "fronts." Parties with varied ideologies sprang up, the most visible and best organized of which was the Russian-inspired Communist Tudeh or "Masses" Party.

Members of the Tudeh in Parliament fought with the factions allied with other countries and often paralyzed the machinery of government. Although we had the rudiments of a democratic parliament, Iranian politicians have never had the Western-style mentality to make it work. They were unskilled and unversed in the arts of political compromise and of "agreeing to disagree" while they carried on the business of running the country. Without a strong authoritarian leader, they reverted to the behavior familiar to the Middle East, an endless shifting of alliances and loyalties that often seems incomprehensible to Western observers.

Almost every month there was a new prime minister appointed by the king, and in this climate, political terrorism became a national pastime. Politicians and a number of journalists were assassinated by terrorists, and after each of these killings there followed a round of accusations and counter-accusations, with each faction accusing the other.

Beginning his reign under these circumstances, my brother was often discouraged by what seemed to be the

46

impossible. He knew that the Allies preferred a weak and ineffectual monarchy, just as foreign powers always had. He knew that if Iran was to survive the war with its borders intact, he had to build at least a semblance of national unity and to create a strong measure of popular support.

But my brother's efforts in this direction were continually subverted by one or another of the foreign powers. At one point, for example, the British Ambassador "suggested" to my brother that he dissolve the Parliament, because the Iranian Prime Minister had told the British that Parliament would vote against the issuance of large amounts of Iranian currency (contrary to law) for use by Allied troops. Naturally, my brother refused, but the British had their way by bringing added pressure to bear on the Shah and on the Parliament (since the British troops were already all too visible in Iran, this was not difficult to do).

As they had a generation before, the Russians consolidated their influence in the northern provinces, not only through the Tudeh Party but also with their armies of occupation. Iran's infant sense of national unity, largely the creation of Reza Khan, was threatening to come apart. There was a return of separatist, tribal thinking.

With the encouragement of the British, who saw the mullahs as an effective counterforce to the Communists, the elements of the extreme religious right were starting to surface again, after years of being suppressed.

The tribal chiefs, once disarmed and politically quiet, also became active and armed again. The Allies had instituted a system of rationing for such scarce items as rice and sugar, and they assigned ration coupons to these chiefs, who were supposed to distribute them to their people. In practice, however, the chiefs often sold the coupons to buy arms, which they then used to regain some of their old autonomy.

It was in the midst of this climate of internal disruption that strange rumors started to circulate in Teheran. These began late in the autumn of 1943, when the radio stopped broadcasting. The official reason given: "technical difficulties." Next, the capital's main telegraph office shut down, and soon after that, no travelers were allowed in or out of the city. Cars and buses headed for Teheran were inexplicably rerouted to nearby cities, and suddenly the streets were filled with Russian, British, and American soldiers carrying machine guns. All the thoroughfares around the British and Russian embassies were blocked by armed soldiers.

There was wild speculation: It was said the new Shah had been arrested. Others believed that Reza Shah had come back from exile and was planning an attack on Iran. There were those who said the Germans had landed forces in Iran. Some insisted that the Russians were conducting intensive searches for German espionage agents. Even one of the newspapers, the only relatively reliable source of information, succumbed to rumor and published a special issue confirming Reza Shah's return to Iran.

Yet the truth behind these extraordinary security measures—the communications blackout and the buildup of troops—was actually more dramatic than the rumors: the heads of the world's greatest powers were all in our country for the Teheran Conference. We were completely unaware that such a conference had been planned or that Teheran had been chosen as the site. I think few people know, even today, all the reasons behind the meeting, but we assumed at the time that it related to some new cooperative Anglo-American-Russian strategies for conducting the final phases of the war.

Whatever the reasons for the conference, it served as an unexpected opportunity for my brother to make his first personal contact with the Allied heads of state. It won for Iran a new friend in Franklin Delano Roosevelt, with whom the Shah talked for several hours. FDR's assurance of American support (no matter how self-serving that turned out to be) made it possible for Iran to stand up to Russia in the years following the war. Stalin, in fact, paid my brother a personal call (only Churchill remained diffident and did not call on the Shah). "Uncle Joe" made very effusive and flattering gestures of friendship and an offer of Russian tanks and planes for Iran's army. But when my brother realized the offer also included Russian officers and other personnel to be sent into Iran, he declined with thanks.

Had he not had such a frank exchange of ideas with Roosevelt, I doubt if he would have been as bold with Stalin. I think Roosevelt appreciated not only the strategic importance of Iran, but also the value of stable relations with a progressive Middle Eastern ruler. (Incidentally, I remember my brother's telling me how surprised he was to see Roosevelt in a wheelchair. Apparently there had been a kind of "gentleman's agreement" in the world press to photograph FDR from the waist up.)

The Teheran Conference lasted for four days, at the end of which two communiqués were issued, on December 1, 1943. In one, the Allied governments recognized "the assistance which Iran has given in the prosecution of the war against the common enemy" and acknowledged that "the war has caused special economic difficulties for Iran." In the light of this, they pledged "to make available to the Government of Iran such economic assistance as may be possible." Furthermore, the Allied governments stated that they were "at one with the Government of Iran in their desire for the maintenance of the independence, sovereignty, and territorial integrity of Iran."

Like the Atlantic Charter, the Teheran communiqué was never fully carried out, at least not by the Soviet Union. Although they were required to leave Iran within six months after the end of the war, they kept their troops in the northwest province of Azerbaijan; and they evacuated Iran only after they had left behind a Communist "democratic republic" created and supported by the Red Army. The creation of this "republic" (in 1945) resulted in prolonged conflict and bloodshed, the effects of which reverberate throughout Iran to this day.

Years after the war some interesting postscripts were written to the Teheran Conference. According to some of the stories that were circulated, there had been a German plan to assassinate the three Allied heads of state during their stay in Teheran. Although we never heard of such a plot, we were aware that Roosevelt, who had first taken up residence in the American Embassy, was quickly moved to the Russian Embassy. Apparently the Russians had "bugged" the American Embassy and were able on the basis of this electronic surveillance to present Roosevelt with evidence of a conspiracy to assassinate him. They convinced the American President to move to the heavily fortified Russian Embassy. In retrospect it seems likely that this show of friendship helped cement the rapport between Roosevelt and Stalin, which, after Yalta, allowed the Russians to extend their influence in Eastern Europe.

In another post-conference incident, it was found that the German Ambassador to Turkey somehow had received copies of all the Teheran Conference secret documents. It turned out that the secretary to the British Ambassador in Turkey was a well-known German agent with the code name of Cicero; he had gained access to his employer's safe and photographed all its contents. Some of these documents revealed an Allied plan to force Turkey into the war. When the German ambassador revealed this plot to Turkish officials, the Turkish government decided to remain neutral, which it did until the February of 1945, when there was no longer any doubt of an Allied victory.

My own feeling—after the fact, of course—is that the most significant aftermath of the Teheran Conference was the friendship between Stalin and Roosevelt, a political misalliance that would give Stalin the green light to begin his infiltration of Eastern Europe and the Middle East.

Those early war years following my father's exile brought radical changes in my own life. Although we were living through a time of anxiety and stress, the presence of so many foreigners in Teheran also made this a time of discovery.

The pace of the city quickened, and all around us there was the sound of different languages and different music, the expression of foreign customs and ideas. Although I am reserved and have had a limited number of close personal relationships, I've always had an ardent curiosity about other people, about how they live and what they think and feel. In the absence of my father's strict hold over us, and in the extremes of wartime conditions, I was free to plan my own days, to take in the sights and sounds around me, to meet new people and exchange ideas, to learn more about the complex and varied world outside of Iran.

My father's exile also meant that the Teymourtash family—and my old friend Mehrpur—could return to Teheran. With Mehrpur, his brother Houshang, and a small circle of friends, I would have, for the first time in my life, a social life outside the royal family. I suppose that the things we did, such as listening to music, dancing, talking about world news, seemed quite tame by Western standards, especially since we were usually chaperoned by my older half-sister; there were limits to which Iranian standards of respectability could be pushed without adding the problem of a royal scandal to my brother's already heavy burden. But compared with the life I had before, those days seemed quite adventuresome.

Before the arrival of the American soldiers, the only music we had known was French and Iranian. Now the

51

Americans established their own radio station as part of their military installation at Amirabad, in the northwestern district of Teheran. We were introduced to the sounds of popular music and the exotic variations of Dixieland and jazz. Houshang became our resident expert on foreign music, and he would often bring us new records to play on our old-fashioned Victrola so we could experiment with the intricacies of Western dances like the fox-trot and the current rage then, the lindy.

The American military base drew a variety of performers who came to entertain the troops. As a budding movie buff (in later years I would see almost every good French and American film made), I was delighted when Fredric March came to Teheran and accepted an invitation to one of our parties. But even more alluring was our introduction to the American sense of humor.

Fascinated as I was by so much of Western culture, I knew I couldn't stay away when I heard that two famous American comedians, Bob Hope and Danny Kaye, would be entertaining the troops at the Amirabad installation. Admission to these events was by special pass, and while I suppose it would have been easy for the Shah's sister to have one of these passes, I wanted very much to have a night out without the fuss and bother of official protocol. So I just tagged along with friends who somehow had managed to get hold of passes, and we were able to lose ourselves in the large crowd that turned out that evening.

Although I couldn't understand all of the comedians' jokes, I found the soldiers' laughter so infectious, I had a wonderful time myself. Compared with the rigid discipline of the Iranian troops, the camaraderie among the American soldiers seemed relatively warm and relaxed. It struck me then, as it would many times in later years, that there were fundamental differences between people who had been born and raised in Western democratic traditions and those who had not been exposed to that kind of culture before. My wartime experiences would increase my curiosity about America, a country that seemed so profoundly different from ours.

In the course of those evenings with my friends I started to think about love. As chaste as these social gatherings were, there was the assumption that someday I would marry Mehrpur. Although I had been married, I was still a stranger to love and passion and all those feelings that inspire poets, songwriters, and adolescent girls. One thing I did know was the extent of my feelings for Mehrpur: they were friendly and affectionate, but they were not feelings of love. To my dismay, in fact, I found that the more time I spent in the company of Mehrpur and his brother, the more I was drawn to his brother Houshang. I was attracted to Houshang's tall good looks, his flamboyant charm, the sophistication he had acquired during his years at school in England. I knew that in this fun-loving, life-loving man I had found my first love. What I would do about this love was a mystery to me. In our culture, women didn't make romantic overtures to men, especially not to men whose brothers they were expected to marry.

One evening, as my friends and I were gathered at my sister's house waiting for Mehrpur to arrive, we received a phone call. It was Mehrpur. "I've had an accident with my car," he said. "I'm calling from the hospital, but there's nothing to worry about."

We understood that Mehrpur's injuries had been slight. A few days later, as we were preparing to go to the hospital to celebrate his recovery and bring him home, we had another phone call, this one telling us that Mehrpur was dead—suddenly—of a blood clot that had developed without warning.

In a strange way, the grief we felt over Mehrpur's death brought Houshang and me together. We talked quietly, reminiscing, saying the kind of things people say to comfort themselves and each other. I soon sensed a difference in

Houshang's mood, and one day, even before he said the words, I knew he was going to tell me he loved me. No one had ever talked to me about love before, and I had never known anyone I wanted to share those feelings with. When Houshang started to talk to me about marriage, the prospect of a life with a man I loved seemed almost intoxicating, especially after the six unhappy years I had spent as the wife of a man I had never cared for.

I wanted to share my happiness with my family, but when I told my brother about my feelings for Houshang, he shook his head and told me it was wrong to become involved with a family that had once betrayed the Pahlavis. I understood what he was saying, but it seemed so unfair. I continued to see Houshang, though all we could do was talk in circles, trying to think of a way we could be together.

"Talk to your brother again" he urged. "Surely you can convince him that I have nothing to do with my father's political views. Doesn't he want you to be happy?"

"Of course," I said to him, "but this isn't a question of happiness. I know my brother. He won't change his mind. He feels I'm wrong even to be considering this marriage."

"Do you think it's wrong for us to love each other?"

"No, of course not," I answered quickly, with a conviction I'm not sure I felt.

"Well, then, it seems to me that we have only one choice. I don't care what your brother says or what your family thinks—it's you I want to marry. We can elope. We can run away and we can make a life of our own. Will you do it?"

I tried to take in all the implications of what Houshang was proposing. To defy my brother and run away with him would create a truly royal scandal in the very proper, very small-town atmosphere of provincial Teheran. My brother would not forgive me, and I would be cut off irretrievably from my own past.

And yet...and yet...I was a woman in love, not just a name on a family tree. Love and affection had not been such abundant emotions in my life that I could walk away from them confident that they would come again. I told Houshang that I would consider his plan.

Several days later, in a state of half-excitement, half-fear, I went to my half-sister's house, where Houshang and I had planned to meet. I was ready to do what he had asked, and I was anxious to see his face when I told him so. He was late, and first I was annoyed with him for keeping me waiting. Then I became frightened, remembering the awful evening we had waited for Mehrpur. Please, God, I prayed over and over again, please let him be all right. Hours passed, and Houshang never came. I gave up my vigil and went home.

There was no word the next day, nor the day after that. I drew my own conclusions: Houshang had changed his mind. Clearly he had thought the whole matter over and decided he did not love me enough. I scolded myself for behaving like an adolescent girl and then I cried, mourning not only the loss of Houshang, but also my romantic, youthful dreams of love.

It was not until two years later, after Houshang had married someone else, that I learned that the scenario behind that last evening was very different from what I had imagined. Realizing how attached I was to Houshang, my brother had sent his friend Ernest Perron to see him. "The Shah doesn't doubt the sincerity of your feelings for his sister," Perron told Houshang, "but His Majesty knows his sister, and he knows that a marriage to you will cause her suffering and unhappiness. If you really love her, you will not attempt to see her again."

By the time I knew the truth, my sense of loss had passed, and I was grateful to my brother for saving me from what I think would have been a tragic mistake. I had believed, for a moment at least, that romantic love could be the basis of a new life for me, but in the years to come I came to think that this warm and rosy glow, lovely though it is, always fades, leaving one to face the problems of stark reality. I would learn I could never embrace any future course at the cost of cutting myself off from my brother.

Yet in the weeks after Houshang went away, I blanketed myself in my private feeling of loss. I decided to leave Iran and visit my father in South Africa. It was a decisive journey, one that led me outside of Iran to other war-torn countries of the world. I met the kinds of people I never thought I would meet. I found dangers that I never could have imagined, and for the first time I did not feel the loneliness and isolation of childhood, but the aloneness of striking out by one's self, the self-reliance that is the mark of independence. (Though self-imposed, I have always considered this voyage to South Africa the first of my three exiles.) When it was over and I returned to Iran, I knew that, at last, I had come into my own.

The first lap of my trip took me from Teheran to Cairo by military airplane. I was warmly received there as a guest of the Egyptian court. In those days Cairo, even at the height of the war, was like an enchanted city, beautiful, mysterious, and exquisitely alive. Against the other capitals of the Middle East, which were just trying to rouse themselves from the darkness of the past, Cairo was like a sparkling jewel: a cosmopolitan city rich with ancient tradition, yet bursting with the intellectual and creative impulses of the twentieth century.

The Abdin Palace, where I stayed, was built in the sprawling linear style of many Eastern palaces, but the interior decor combined the opulence of East and West. Savonnerie carpets, oversize oriental rugs, antique tapestries, and remarkable examples of inlaid ivory work framed a magnificent array of European antiques and *objets d'art*.

In Teheran the royal family lived comfortably but simply, probably no better than a prosperous European family of the *haute bourgeoisie*. But Egyptian court life evoked the glitter and splendor of the oriental fairy tales, with perhaps a *soupçon* of Versailles. Poets, artists, musicians, intellectuals, and aristocrats mingled at lavish balls and soirees, and witty repartee—in English, Turkish, Italian, Arabic, and French— was raised almost to an art form.

I thought the women of the Egyptian court very lovely and fashionable. Whether they had the classic look of Nefertiti or a Western profile inherited from a Western parent, they were dressed and made up exactly like the European women I had seen. But as I spoke to these women about what their lives were really like, I realized that even though the veil had been discarded, its symbolic presence was still felt. Although there were some Egyptian women who pushed their lives beyond the limits of social con- vention, most of them were bound socially and sexually through the same kind of rules that bound Iranian women.

The dominant figure at the court was, of course, my sister-in-law's brother, King Farouk. But this Farouk, the one I came to know, was not the overweight, dissipated monarch who became the subject of so many Western satirists and cartoonists. He was still a handsome young man, lean and tall, patriotic and idealistic, with clear blue eyes that sparkled when he spoke. I sympathized with him when he told me about the frustrations of trying to rule in the shadow of constant, powerful British interference. (Iran had had more than enough of her own frustration with the British.) He complained that each time he tried to make a move that the British considered inimical to their interests, or each time he appointed a prime minister with vocal anti-British views, his palace was ringed with military forces and tanks, which stayed there until he backed down.

From those conversations, I came to believe that this kind of struggle with the British made Farouk feel completely defeated as a man and as a king and led him later to turn to the opiate of nightclubs and casinos.

Politics was not the only subject Farouk discussed with
me. I had visited Cairo briefly once before, with my sister-in-
law Fawzia, and at that time I noticed her brother staring at
me whenever we were in the same room, his eyes lingering
on my face. When we spoke, he paid me lavish compliments
and attentions, above and beyond what courtesy—even
oriental courtesy—would require. During this trip, his attentions intensified, and he gave several gala parties for me
aboard his yacht on the Nile and at his beautiful summer
palace in Alexandria.

It was at one of these parties that Farouk told me—what
I have never before revealed—that he loved me and wanted
to marry me. Before I could remind him that he was already
married, he went on to explain that he no longer loved
Queen Farida and was planning to divorce her. Although I
thought Farouk was an attractive man, I was in no mood to
hear declarations of love, especially not from the husband of
a woman I considered my friend. I tried to discourage
Farouk without hurting his pride.

Nor was Farouk my only suitor. Several Egyptian
princes made overtures which I found flattering, but after
my disappointment with Houshang, I couldn't take any of
them seriously. I did, however, meet the man who later
would become my second husband. It was a clear and balmy
day, and I was galloping my horse on the beautiful grounds
of the Royal Horseriding Club, which sits on an island in the
middle of the Nile. A friend introduced me to Ahmad Shafiq,
the son of Farouk's Minister of Court. Ahmad's mother had
come from the Caucasus, his father from Turkey, and he had
inherited his father's dark hair and his mother's fine features.
As he galloped alongside me, I admired his horsemanship,
his elegant profile, and his sun-bronzed face. During the last
few days of my Egyptian visit I would see Ahmad several
times. His manners were as courtly and elegant as his
appearance, and I liked him in an objective rather than a

personal way, as I would have liked a beautiful painting or a lovely landscape.

Before I left Egypt, Ahmad's sister came to see me (in the Middle East, sisters are often emissaries in affairs of the heart), and in the usual roundabout way she let me know that her brother was fond of me and that I could expect a proposal of marriage. The next step, of course, was to find out, without exactly asking a direct question, how I would respond. I avoided a direct "yes" or "no," telling her instead that I was too preoccupied at the moment with plans to visit my father.

Farouk was at that very moment trying to find a means of transportation that would take me to Johannesburg. Travel was difficult throughout the war, but local British officials agreed to put me on a military plane carrying flight crews south. Flying in those days was an adventure, even on civilian planes, but on a military plane in wartime it was rugged. I boarded the plane and found myself the only woman among 40 soldiers. I spoke no English and they no Persian (this forced me to quickly learn my first English words), but my childhood experiences as "one of the boys" put me at ease—at least until we were in the air; then, like cargo, seated on long wooden benches, we lurched back and forth with every movement of the plane.

We landed at military airports in Khartoum, Nairobi, and Durban, on airstrips that either were made of wire mesh placed on dirt or grass or were just dirt strips. During our stopovers, we spent the nights at British rest houses. I had my meals with the pilot and co-pilot, and each night after dinner they would see me to my room, instruct me to lock my door and windows, and leave me with the warning that "there are Africans around, and who knows what might happen." Apparently the British felt the Africans had a monopoly on antisocial behavior.

When we landed in Johannesburg, it was at an airport

100 kilometers from the city. As soon as I looked out the window, I saw my brother Ali Reza, who had come to meet me and take me by jeep to my father's house. So many years have passed since that trip to South Africa, but I can still remember that big frame house, surrounded by a dense tropical garden, with red, white, and brown bougainvilleas climbing up the walls.

I was delighted to see my father; we hugged and kissed, and before I could get my breath or ask how he was, he barraged me with questions. How was my brother? What was happening in Iran? Before I could finish one answer, he interrupted with another question. When I had finished describing to him everything that had happened since he left, there were tears in his eyes. "May God have mercy on our country," he murmured. "And may He help my son."

The following morning his secretary, a short, plump man with a round face and a strong sense of loyalty, came to me and said; "His Majesty wants to see you."

I went immediately to the study, where my father was waiting for me. "Do you remember the last day in Isfahan?" he asked. "Remember what I told you when you asked to come here with me? Your brother needed you then, and from what I've heard from you and other sources, I feel you shouldn't stay away from Iran too long. I would love to keep you here, but travel is difficult, and I think we must begin to look for a way to send you back."

I had planned on staying with my father for at least a few months, but I agreed with him that I had a responsibility to my brother. Finding passage home was even more difficult than it had been in getting here. Since the war had spread to Japan and the Pacific, both air and sea routes were hazardous. Every day my brother Ali Reza and my father's secretary went to Johannesburg and made inquiries, without success, at various public and private travel agencies. It would be almost six weeks before they would find a way for me to leave Africa.

In the meantime I spent my days in my father's garden playing tennis with Ali Reza and an Englishman who lived nearby. I hadn't played so often and so long since childhood days, and in spite of the hot African sun I could feel my muscles and reflexes responding as I pushed them a little harder each day. After one particularly hard and fast set (which I won), my British partner said: "You know, young lady, you're really quite good. How would you like to play at Wimbledon? I could arrange it if you're interested."

My competitive spirits were immediately aroused. For anyone interested in sports, Wimbledon was one of those legendary names one always associates with being "best." Immediately I ran to my father to ask permission, but he seemed angry that I would even raise such a question. "Have you forgotten already?" he asked. "It was the British who sent me into exile. How can you even think about going to their country to play tennis?" And that, as usual, was the end of the discussion.

In the evenings Ali Reza and I would sometimes go into Johannesburg to see an English or American film. My favorite actors in those days were Gary Cooper and Clark Gable. Having been raised by a "larger than life" father who was the very embodiment of traditional masculine characteristics, I think I've always been drawn to these qualities, in real life as well as on the stage and screen.

Ali Reza was very much that kind of man. At 22, he was strong-willed, courageous in the same flamboyant and daredevil way my father had been. When all of us children were together, I inevitably chose to spend time with my twin; but here, during the weeks in Africa, I came to appreciate my "little brother" (he was three years younger than we). He could be great fun when he was happy, and like many really strong men, he could be very generous and giving of himself. If I had known how short a time Ali Reza would spend on this earth, I think I would have treasured the days I had with him even more. Some ten years later, in

61

1954, he flew toward home from a hunting trip on the Caspian shores, piloting a small plane himself over the Alborz Mountains. He never reached Teheran for the Shah's birthday celebration (and mine), and it was eight days before we found his body in the mountains.

Ali Reza and I explored Johannesburg, which, with its tall buildings and broad attractive streets, resembled many European cities. But the beauty of the city was marred by the cruel and highly visible signs of segregation. Theaters, restaurants, parks, beaches, and even sidewalks were segregated. To do the day's shopping, a housewife had to take her place on either the "Coloured" or "White" side of the wall that divided the grocery store. This made a deep and lasting impression on me, one that many years later, during my first term at the UN, would draw me directly to the Human Rights Commission, where my first speech would deal with racial discrimination in South Africa.

For the moment, our concern was for Iran and my brother, and as we had done so many times before, Father, Ali Reza, and I would gather around the radio to hear the news on the BBC; this was our principal source of news, since telegrams were censored and newspapers took several weeks to arrive. Often, when the news was sketchy—making my father very impatient—I would finish the evening by reading to him. One of the books I read from regularly was a translation of the British Foreign Ministry's Blue Book. For a bookmark, I used a signed photograph of Ahmad Shafiq. One evening, as I sat down to read, I noticed the picture wasn't where I had left it. I flipped through the whole book quickly, but I just couldn't find it. I carried on with my reading, not wanting to ask my father about the photo, but later, as we were talking, he said; "I don't like the idea of my children marrying foreigners."

His message was brief but very clear, so I never brought up my visit to Egypt or my proposal from Ahmad Shafiq. Instead, I changed the subject to the news that my father's secretary had brought us: he had located the captain of a cargo ship that would be carrying ammunition and other war supplies toward the Suez Canal. The captain had said he would be willing to take me aboard, providing I understood that he couldn't guarantee my safety and that I would be traveling at my own risk. My father left the decision to me, and after I weighed the danger involved against the chance that I wouldn't find other transportation, I said I would go to the seaport of Durban to meet the ship.

Before I left, my father took me aside, and in a voice that shook with emotion, he said: "I know you can be strong, but I want you always to be strong for your brother. Stay close to him and tell him to stand firm in the face of dangers of any kind." As I gave my assurances to my father, I realized how old a man he had become, that he was no longer in very good health, and I might not ever see him again. I looked hard at his face, trying to memorize the features that were still imposing even though they had softened a little with age—it was the last time I would see them. On July 26, 1944, six months after I left Johannesburg, my father died of heart disease, at the age of 69.

The house where he lived in Africa became a museum, housing his personal effects and the memorabilia of his career. Since the 1979 revolution these may well be the only things of his that remain, though in a larger sense there is something of Reza Shah in everything he built in Iran.

Ali Reza drove me from Johannesburg to Durban, where we arrived just in time for a quick good-bye before I boarded the ship. I introduced myself to the captain, a tall heavy man with a flourishing brown mustache and curly red hair. Although the ship had no passenger facilities, the captain graciously gave me his cabin and tried his best to make me feel at home on this vessel loaded with war supplies and sailors.

Since we were carrying munitions, the atmosphere on

the ship was tense, the crew subdued, none of them knowing if we would reach our destination. A few days out of Durban, the captain came to see me, with bad news written all over his face. "I'm very sorry, Your Highness, I have something to tell you..." he trailed off, obviously unhappy about what he had to say.

"Come on," I urged him. "Tell me. What's wrong."

"Enemy submarines have been sighted in this area, Your Highness. I will have to put in at Mombasa in Kenya and I have been instructed to drop you off there."

"You can't do that," I protested, imagining myself stranded in Africa for the duration of the war. "I must get back to Iran. You can't just leave me in a strange port where I don't know a soul." I knew even as I argued that the captain really didn't have a choice.

"I'm sorry," he said, trying to be reassuring. "You won't be left all alone, Your Highness. I've sent a cable to the governor of Mombasa informing him of your arrival. He'll send someone to meet you. Don't worry, I'm sure you'll get home soon."

When we arrived at Mombasa, I found it to be quite a lovely city, almost as European in flavor as Johannesburg. Everywhere, along the wide boulevards and flanking the tall, stately buildings, there were carefully laid out rows of tropical trees and densely massed clusters of exotic flowers. I was met by the governor's representative, who drove me to a British rest house in Nairobi. My first impression of Nairobi was surprising. I didn't know a great deal about Africa, but I hadn't expected such beautiful residential areas, such clean, brightly colored houses invariably surrounded with plants and flowers. In Teheran, although the plants and flowers are fresh and bright in early spring, the scarcity of rain makes them dull and dusty the rest of the year, so to me the year-round bloom of Africa's plant life was a constant source of pleasure.

About 50 kilometers outside of Nairobi I drove through the low grass of the wildlife preserve. All around us there were lions, giraffes, wild animals so close one could reach out and touch them, so free and beautiful that they touched the heart in some indefinable way. Yet as hauntingly beautiful as I found Kenya, I still wanted to leave as quickly as I could. One afternoon, as I was sipping a glass of lemonade in the lobby of my rest house, a young man—tall, blond, wearing a white shirt and blue slacks and carrying a small briefcase—came in and stood in front of me. Seeing me sitting alone, he asked if he might join me. His English was easy to understand, and by now I had learned at least enough English to manage a conversation. "What's a young lady like you doing alone in Africa?" he asked me almost at once.

He seemed like a decent man, so I explained how I had ended up in Nairobi and why I needed to find transportation to Cairo. In turn, he told me that he was a pilot who owned a small plane which he used for crop-dusting. Suddenly our meeting seemed like an act of divine providence. I invited the young man to dinner.

Over dinner I put my proposition to him: If he would let me charter his plane for a trip north, I would pay him twice what he could earn on a crop-dusting expedition. He looked at me incredulously and burst into laughter. "Look, miss," he said, "I don't think you understand. All I have is a small, single-engine plane. It can't carry more than a hundred pounds, and I'm not at all sure it can fly that distance."

Having found a pilot and a plane, no matter what size, I wasn't ready to give up so easily. I coaxed, I cajoled, I threw myself on the young pilot's mercy. "Okay, okay," he said. "This is going to be a challenge for my plane and for me. But I'm telling you right now, you can't carry any luggage, and I can take you only as far as the Sudanese border." We shook hands, and I went off to get a good night's sleep.

The next morning I packed whatever I could fit into my shoulder bag and left all my other things behind. The weather was bright and sunny—reassuring, after I had a look at the flimsy crop-duster. My pilot friend told me that he intended to carry on with his work as we made our way north. It was a fantastic flight—ten days in that tiny plane, since we had to land often near small villages to replenish our fuel and insecticide supplies. In these small villages I saw for the first time an Africa that wasn't the creation of Europeans, a primitive Africa of simple huts inhabited by natives who painted their naked bodies with the brightest of nature's colors.

Our last stop was at a village in the middle of a forest, on the bank of a branch of the Nile. "This village isn't far from Jobo," the pilot explained, as he escorted me to a British rest house. "I'll introduce you to a friend of mine as soon as we arrive. He's a reliable man, and I'm sure he'll help you get to Khartoum."

The friend was a German painter and author who had come to Africa to get away from war and bloodshed and the decadent civilization of Europe. "Here in Africa," he told me, "I can feel close to nature and to people who have not been corrupted." He showed me some of the paintings he had done for a book he was writing on African life.

My newest "home away from home" was a village that consisted of a few small huts on the river bank. The people lived a very relaxed, very basic kind of life, unhurried and only slightly structured. Grownups and children alike seemed to spend much of the day frolicking and swimming in the muddy waters of the river. After one of these romps in the river, the small children would emerge from the water, their skins transformed from black to brown. All of these people were warm and friendly, but communication was difficult, limited mainly to broad gestures, since neither the German painter nor I could speak the local dialect.

Actually, the communication between the painter and me wasn't always successful either, given my limited German vocabulary and his limited fluency in French. This heightened my feeling of being stranded in the middle of nowhere, and my usually strong sense of determination started to flag.

Within a few days of my arrival, however, some Europeans living in nearby villages heard about the peripatetic Iranian princess, and they came to meet me. Their kindness diminished the feeling of isolation, and soon we were like old friends. Every night a few of them would come to visit, and we would communicate through the almost universal language of bridge, or would talk about how I might be able to continue my journey.

There were no roads in our area, and the Europeans who owned jeeps used them only for short trips to nearby villages. For longer trips, one had to travel by small plane or go up the Nile by boat. One evening, as we all sat around talking, the German painter started to joke: "You don't have to worry," he said. "You've become so popular in this area that we all consider you our queen. To make our queen happy, my friends and I are willing to take you to Khartoum or even Cairo on a boat. We'll row all the way if we have to."

I seized upon his joke. "Why can't we do that?" I asked. "Seriously, do you think we can find a boat? If I am your queen, then that is my royal command." We all laughed, but the painter promised to try to locate a boat.

Although I realized that there might be a long wait between the time we adopted this plan and the day we might actually leave, I felt much better for just having a plan. My German friend started making maps and charts and lists of supplies we would need, and I tried to find some news of Iran on a borrowed battery-operated radio.

The Germans seemed to be completely on the defensive under the constant pressure of Allied bombing. In Italy their defense line in Monte Cassino was broken, while the Russians were successfully throwing the German troops back. About Iran, there was very little, and I assured myself that in wartime no news was probably good news.

My thoughts raced ahead to the day the war would end. The Allies had promised to leave Iran after the war—but would they? The strategic considerations—and the oil—that brought them to Iran originally might be even more attractive in a postwar setting. Might the big powers agree, as they had before, to divide Iran?

The divisions that had resurfaced after the Allied occupation and my father's exile could destroy Iran's prospects for an independent, prosperous, and progressive future. We had the means for such a future: we were rich in natural resources, we were not overpopulated, and our people, though uneducated and untrained, were certainly intelligent and industrious enough to create a solid bridge between the Persia of their parents' day and a new Iran for their children.

But if this was to happen, I felt it was critical for Iran to present a united national front to the rest of the world and to build, as soon as possible, an army capable of defending our borders. Whatever the dangers from the outside, I felt that a strong nationalism had to take its place beside religious beliefs as the dominant faith maker.

What Iran needed—how clear this was to me as I waited thousands of miles away in Africa to return home—was practical, pragmatic secular planning. We needed to educate our people to the value of a central government. Without such a government there would never be peace and stability. And we very much needed the help and support of intelligent, progressive—and loyal—politicians. But who?

I was impatient to get home and discuss all these issues with my brother. The days in that African village were hot and humid and very slow in passing. Fortunately the rest house had ceiling fans and an ice-making machine, powered by a generator that made an infernal racket. We were grateful all the same for anything that gave relief from the heat, especially since the polluted water, which had to be boiled before it could be used for drinking, was always tepid. Since I had arrived in the village with only the clothes on my back, I was very touched when one of the native women made me a shirt of the tropical khaki material the European men used. This gave me one change of clothing that I could wash and try to dry, though everything got hot and sticky almost within minutes of my putting it on.

The nights were a little better, and every evening my new friends and I gathered in the big dining room of the rest house to talk about our proposed trip up the Nile. Some said it was a foolish idea, fraught with dangers and risks I couldn't imagine. But I confess these arguments did very little to discourage me. I have always been fascinated by the mystery and romance of rivers, perhaps because we have no great rivers in Iran. Even now, in exile, I love to watch the East River from my bedroom window, tamed though it is, and dominated by the smokestacks and the harsh neon signs of old factories.

The Nile, however—that was another story. Even today the Nile has not been demystified. I had seen it only from my room in the Abdin Palace or from the royal yacht; but I had read stories about adventurous explorers who had mounted expeditions to find the source of that great river, and so I tried to convince my companions that the trip could be a sizeable challenge and an adventure. Yet before we found a suitable boat that could make the voyage, one of the men in our group brought the news that a small plane had arrived in our area and that the pilot was willing to fly me as far as Khartoum. Excited as I was at the chance to get home, I couldn't really regret giving up the Nile expedition (and I'm sure my friends weren't really sorry to forgo the adventure).

On the day of my departure, all the villagers, as well as the German painter and his friends, came to see me off. We said our good-byes like old friends, and I tried to thank these warm and generous people for taking me in and offering such comfort and hospitality to a stranger. There were tears in my eyes as my plane took off and as they called out farewells, waving their handkerchiefs under the hot African sun.

At Khartoum Airport, I was surprised to find a British colonel waiting for me. Apparently the pilot had radioed ahead, for the colonel saluted smartly and said: "Welcome to Khartoum, Your Highness. I've been assigned by the Governor-General of Sudan to greet you and escort you to his palace. The Governor-General invites you to be his guest for the duration of your stay here." When we arrived at the palace, the Governor-General and his wife were waiting for me at the top of the stairs. Limp and bedraggled—I was still dressed in my khaki shirt—I was touched and a little embarrassed by this formal welcome.

My new hosts promptly showed me to a very comfortable room, which seemed absolutely luxurious after what I had become accustomed to in those African villages. The Governor-General's palace was a two-story British colonial-style villa, set in the middle of hundreds of the ubiquitous bougainvillea bushes. The Governor himself looked exactly as if he had stepped out of a movie about an English colonial governor. He had a tall, lean, aristocratic look, blond hair parted in the middle, a pale, narrow mustache gracing his upper lip. When he spoke, it was with the carefully modulated tones and clipped accent of the upper class, with his head tilted to one side and the words issuing from the opposite side of his mouth.

He and his wife lived in that gracious, formal style that characterized the last days of the Empire. Meals were formal affairs at which everyone dressed (the day after my arrival the Governor arranged for a woman companion to take me shopping for some clothes) and at which food was elegantly prepared and served elaborately by Sudanese servants. The dominant subject of mealtime conversation was the war. At that time, the spring of 1944, everyone was speculating about the possibility of a "third front." The Americans had taken New Guinea, the Russians had entered Romania, and the German war machine seemed to be paralyzed by Allied bombing. But the Governor took the cautious and conservative view that a war cannot be considered won until it is actually over. He felt that the Japanese were capable of prolonged and tenacious resistance that might drag on for months or even years.

About the future of the British Empire, however, the Governor seemed remarkably sanguine. He pointed to the fact that soldiers of the Commonwealth countries were at that moment fighting bravely for Britain on many fronts all over the world. He added that the domestic situation in the Sudan was stable and secure, and he was, for the moment, quite right.

I stayed about two weeks in Khartoum, and in spite of my impatience, the time was pleasantly spent. The Governor's palace had a swimming pool and a tennis court, which I couldn't resist for very long. It wasn't Wimbledon, but in a local tournament I did finish first among the women and second among the men.

What I still remember most about that visit is the picturesque setting of the city, which was like an oasis adjoining the Nile. The strong desert winds constantly spread a film of fine sand everywhere, and in spite of the heavily insulated doors and windows, there was always the dry, gritty taste of sand in one's mouth. And it is here one sees the two branches of the Nile, the "white" (actually rather muddy) and the "blue," come together.

Thanks to the Governor-General's intercession, the British government gave special permission for a military plane to take me to Cairo. The same colonel who welcomed me to Khartoum came to drive me to the airport in a military car. Several miles before we reached our destination, we saw great clouds of smoke coming from the direction of the airport. When we reached the gate, the colonel said he would investigate. After a quarter hour or so he came back and said very calmly: "I'm sorry to inform you that the plane scheduled to take you to Cairo is on fire. The smoke we saw was from that plane."

I was quite astonished by this example of British understatement. In the Middle East, news of this kind would usually be delivered with many dramatic flourishes and embellishments. I was tremendously disappointed by this new delay, but in the face of the colonel's calm reserve, I felt I shouldn't say anything.

When I returned to the Governor's palace I was warmly welcomed once again, with a few jokes about my situation. The Governor-General informed me that the fire was not caused by sabotage, but by a leak in the plane's fuel tank. "You were really quite fortunate, dear lady," he said. "If you had actually taken off, the aircraft undoubtedly would have exploded in midair."

Two days later I boarded another military aircraft, uneventfully this time. For the first time since I had come to Africa, I found myself on a solid, reliable means of transportation. Undoubtedly my distant ancestors must have made similar long, tortuous journeys by caravan, but I felt more relaxed and at home with this direct and efficient form of travel.

As we headed toward Cairo, I felt as if I had lived through a long and fascinating travelogue of a journey shared with so many people—a ship's captain and dozens of sailors, the young pilot, the German painter, the people of the little villages, the Governor-General and his wife— against a background of the most exotic flora and fauna I had ever seen. It is odd to think of how people who are complete strangers can come together briefly, share a small portion of their lives, and then separate forever. I imagined, as I flew toward Cairo, that the pilot was probably dusting another field, the German painter sketching one of his village scenes, the native villagers swimming in the Nile—and, too, I carried with me that last image of my father, his face worn, his eyes intense as he ordered me to tell my brother not to be afraid.

At Cairo military airport I was met by King Farouk and Queen Farida. No sooner had I settled into the Abdin Palace than Farouk again started talking about love and marriage. Ahmad Shafiq renewed his suit, too, and I had to be careful, for Ahmad's sake, to keep his intentions hidden from the king.

I noticed that Farouk seemed even more demoralized about the British presence and more detached from the business of ruling his country than when we had last met. Although the British had saved Africa from the Nazis, Farouk no longer had any hope that after the war he would be rid of British interference.

There were rumors that Farouk was having a discreet affair with a teenage middle-class girl called Narriman, and Queen Farida, who had also heard these rumors, asked for my advice. Farida had three daughters, but she had not been fortunate enough to bear a son. Having long since made up my mind that I would do nothing to add to Farida's marital problems, I tried to console her by saying that Farouk's interest in Narriman was probably superficial and would pass in time. But since Farouk seemed to have lost interest in Farida, and since there was yet to be a male heir, I didn't see much hope that their marriage would last much longer.

As for my own situation with Ahmad Shafiq, I had mixed feelings. I knew I didn't love him, but the more I saw him, the more I liked him. He was not only good-looking and urbane, he was also serious and hard-working, a self-made man (he managed the financial department of a sugar factory), and these were qualities I admired. We had one long, serious conversation before I left Cairo, in which I tried to be frank and honest about my feelings while leaving the door open on the subject of marriage.

It should be added that after my departure Farouk turned more and more to Narriman. He decided to separate from Farida, but he faced a serious dilemma. At that time he would have been the first modern Muslim king to divorce his queen, and this would no doubt have had unpleasant repercussions since Farida was quite popular in Egypt.

Unexpectedly, circumstances gave Farouk the solution he was looking for when Fawzia made one of her frequent trips to Egypt. It was clear that she preferred the court life of Cairo to that of Teheran, and this time her visit extended from weeks into months. Each time my brother asked her to return, she found another excuse not to do so. Finally—and this must have been with Farouk's encouragement in order to pave the way to end his own marriage—she asked my brother for a divorce. (Contrary to popular rumor, it was not the Shah who had initiated the divorce because Fawzia had failed to produce a male heir.)

The Shah resisted, but when he realized that Fawzia was adamant about staying in Cairo, he agreed to the end of the marriage. It was hard for me to be angry with her, even though she behaved in this way. I thought of her as a tame cat that adapts better to a familiar environment than to a new one. Once she had returned to Cairo and resettled there, I think the easiest course for her was to stay, even if it meant leaving behind her husband and baby daughter.

After terms of the divorce had been finalized, Fawzia married an Egyptian army officer. As far as I know she was content with her new life, which was a quiet and simple one. After Farouk was deposed, she and her husband moved to a modest house on the outskirts of Cairo. Our family kept in touch with her, and after her brother lost the throne, we helped her financially and arranged for her to visit her daughter Princess Shahnaz in Switzerland.

## · V ·

# THE BLACK PANTHER

My first weeks back in Teheran were hectic ones. The political confusion I had left behind when I went to Africa worsened during the final months of the war. I was convinced that the perceptions I had had while I was away were correct ones, that this must be a time of decisive action for Iran. Most of our family was in exile, Fawzia had left for Cairo, and my brother and I were left alone. Since there were few people my brother could trust and rely on, and since I had promised my father I would stand by him, I began my career on the domestic political scene—but unofficially, as the constitution forbids members of the royal family to hold political office.

I had often thought, during the months in Africa, of how much we needed a means of reaching the people and mobilizing popular support for my brother. A strong, well-produced newspaper seemed to be one of the answers, and I met with an experienced editor who said he could produce such a paper with financial assistance. After a talent search for skilled professional journalists and writers, of which there were few in Iran, we developed an organization that would create an evening daily that became the most widely read evening newspaper in Iran.

My first priority, however, was to make political friends for the regime and to neutralize some of the opposition. Every day I met unofficially with individuals and groups representing various points of view. I listened to them and tried to convince them that Iran badly needed a viable central government and a greater national unity. As a result of these personal discussions and exchanges, I hoped it might be possible to consolidate and integrate some of these factions and thereby gain a broad base of support for the monarchy.

This involvement of mine in politics generated a well-oiled rumor machine which regularly turned out stories linking my hand with government issues of all sorts—everything from petty incidents to the assassination of high officials. These rumors were so persistent that they crossed our borders, and soon European newspapers christened me "The Power Behind the Throne" and "The Black Panther of Iran."

Looking back on this postwar period, I almost have to smile when I think of the convoluted, almost superhuman feats of manipulation that were attributed to me. While it is certainly true that our Middle Eastern politics often seem terribly Byzantine to the Western observer, I was at that time a young woman still in my twenties with much more energy and determination than experience (my brother and I together did not have more than a half-century of living behind us).

Actually, I think it was the fact that I was a woman working actively in politics, then an exclusively male domain, which raised eyebrows and set tongues wagging. My activities in this world of men also started to fuel stories about my personal life. To squelch these stories, my brother suggested that I marry and put an end at least to the more scandalous rumors. (I did marry, but the rumors didn't end.)

76

Although I had no particular wish to find another husband, I had come to terms with the reality that for a princess, marriage was not necessarily an emotional, private affair. I wasn't in love with anyone, and my prospects were limited to the Egyptian princes who had expressed an interest in my hand and, of course, to Ahmad Shafiq. Since I was being asked to choose a husband at that point, I chose Ahmad Shafiq, whom I admired and liked.

But when I sent word to Ahmad that I accepted his proposal, I found that any wedding plans would have to wait. Farouk was apparently still smarting from a bad case of wounded royal pride; I had not only turned down his proposal, but now I was accepting that of another Egyptian, a man of lower social rank. He refused to give my fiancé a passport to leave Egypt.

So I had no choice but to return to Egypt myself, accompanied by Nasrollah Entezam, Iran's Chief of Protocol, who later served as chairman of the UN General Assembly and as Iran's ambassador to France. My second wedding was a "no-frills" affair, held without pomp or circumstance at the Iranian Embassy in Cairo, but it was still a happier occasion than the day of my first wedding. If I didn't have stars in my eyes, I did have a handsome, charming husband, and the hope that we might make a life together based on friendship and mutual respect. Farouk expressed his continued hostility to my marriage by not sending a congratulatory note or flowers (in a part of the world where the rituals of courtesy are observed regardless of personal feelings, this was an expression of hostility directed at my entire family), but he could no longer refuse to grant my legal husband a passport without severing political relations between his country and mine.

In spite of the quality of abrasiveness in our relationship, I think I always had lingering feelings of compassion for Farouk, for the patriotic idealist he once was and for the king he might have been. As is well known, Farouk's reign ended in 1952, by a military coup which had the tacit support of the Americans (Nasser, Najib, and Abdu Latif Baghdadi, along with several others, met with the U.S. military attaché in Cairo before the coup). Farouk resigned quietly and was sent, aboard the royal yacht, into exile in Italy. He had by now married Narriman and, ironically, Farouk had had the son and heir he had wanted for so long.

When my new husband and I returned to Teheran, we went right to work, each of us in a different area. Shafiq was a hard-working, intelligent businessman, and soon after our arrival in Iran he established with his own family funds a small civil airline called Pars. With a few chartered airplanes, he initiated regular flights between Teheran and Paris, as well as several domestic routes. This company, which was later bought for a nominal fee by the government, became the nucleus for National Iran Airways—Iranair—one of the most successful international airlines at the time of the recent revolution.

After my marriage I began my work in the field of social welfare. I had inherited about $300,000 when my father died (and about 1 million square meters of land near the Caspian Sea, as well as properties in Gorgan and Kermanshah, which would later become extremely valuable), so I used about $15,000 of my own funds to found the "Social Services Foundation." I persuaded a group of well-educated Iranian women to use their energies and abilities to help me carry out several welfare programs.

Although the Islamic religion makes it mandatory for each person to help his less fortunate brethren, the actuality of a government machinery capable of implementing this ideal was pioneered in the West, and fairly recently at that. Even so, in spite of our lower standard of living, we in Iran have had a more highly developed sense of being "our brother's keeper." While I feel this sense of mutuality and caring ranks much higher as a human value than the cold

*Family picture: My father, Reza Khan, with (from left to right) my twin brother Mohammed Reza, my sister Shams and me (3 years old)*

*Water carrier in Teheran in the early twentieth century*

*A Persian couple of the same period*

*Muslim theater depicting the death of the martyrs of our religion*

*Kebab sellers in old Teheran*

*My father, Reza Khan (left), and a friend in the uniform of the Persian Cossack Brigade*

*My father and my brother, the Crown Prince, clocking the Trans-Iranian Railway*

*Arrival in Khorramshahr of my brother and his new bride, Fawzia. Front row: Egypt's Queen Mother Nazli and my mother, Taj-ol-Muluk. Second row: Fawzia, my sister Shams, myself, and Fawzia's sister, Faiza*

*Turkey's President Ataturk greeting my father, Reza Shah*

*My brother and myself, age 14, at Le Rosey*

*School photograph of the soccer team at Le Rosey.*
*My brother, team captain is seated, center front; his childhood friend,*
*Hussein Fardust, standing, extreme left*

*My father and I during his exile in Johannesburg, South Africa*

*My sister Shams, my late brother Ali Reza, and I*

*With my sister-in-law Fawzia (left) in the garden at Saadabad*

*With my first son Shahram*

*Iranians unloading cargo during the Allied occupation in World War II*

*Truck convoy carrying supplies through Iran to Russia*

*Trans-Iranian Railway becomes
part of the Allied supply line to Russia*

*Azerbaijan in December 1945. One day after the proclamation of the
Communist "republic," Soviet-type uniforms appeared in the streets*

*My brother, his wife Fawzia, and their daughter Shahnaz*

*Iranian Prime Minister Haj Ali Razmara*

*Wedding photograph of my brother and his second wife, Soraya*

*The Shah with President Harry Truman during a visit to the United States*

*The Shah being greeted by President Dwight D. Eisenhower in Washington*

*My half-sister Fatemeh, myself, and Prime Minister Jawaharlal Nehru during one of my trips to Kashmir*

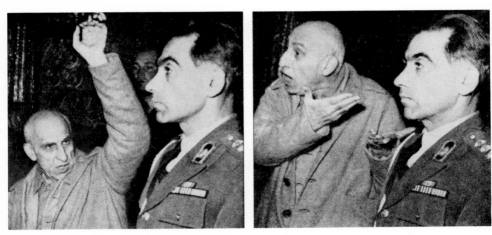

*Defendant Mohammed Mossadegh curses defense counsel in the course of his trial following his attempted coup in 1953*

*A quarter million Americans turn out to welcome the Shah to New York in 1948*

**Newsweek**

JUNE 26, 1961 25c

**Shah of Iran: A Revolution From the Top?**

*The Shah at the height of his reign,* Newsweek, *June 26, 1961 (Copyright 1961 by Newsweek, Inc. All rights reserved. Reprinted by permission)*

FIFTEEN CENTS

**TIME**

THE WEEKLY NEWSMAGAZINE

IRAN'S REZA SHAH PAHLAVI
He played both ends until they met.
(World War)

*His Majesty, Reza Shah, at the time of the Allied occupation,* Time, *September 8, 1941 (Reprinted by permission from TIME, The Weekly Newsmagazine; copyright Time Inc. 1941)* and anonymous distribution of charity often found in the West, we had, nevertheless, an aching need for some sort of organized welfare in Iran.

Many of our people did not have the means to help themselves, let alone their relatives, no matter how much they wanted to. The first time I went into the Teheran slums to see for myself what kind of help was most needed, I literally became ill. I had always known—at least intellectually—that there were people less fortunate than I, people who could not take for granted a comfortable place to live, enough to eat, and clothes to wear, but I had never seen with my own eyes the kind of day-to-day misery that breeds apathy and despair. Never had I seen so many people jammed into such small, filthy quarters, with so little to sustain or cover or nourish them.

When I took a jeep into some of the remote provincial villages, I found conditions that were no less grim. In those rural villages it was not unusual for a whole family to live on the yield of a date tree and a pair of scrawny goats. Living on the barest subsistence level, these people had no buffers at all against any form of natural disaster, such as epidemic, earthquake, or drought. It was not unusual in those villages to hear old people discuss the past in terms like "the year of the famine" or "the year of the cholera."

Since we felt our infant welfare organization could be more effective in more accessible areas like Teheran, my co-workers and I started our programs in the city. Each day we would go to the slum areas in the south of the city and operate a soup kitchen, distributing hot meals and clothing. We also established a pediatric clinic in the same area.

As soon as these first programs were operating smoothly, I began looking for ways to expand the organization; it later became the Imperial Organization for Social Services, the largest social agency in Iran. I enlisted the help of an old friend, Abdolhossein Hajir, who was the Minister of Finance. Hajir was an intelligent and compassionate man with an excellent grasp of historical and political perspectives, as well as a striking personal appearance—he was tall and slender and always wore sunglasses to camouflage an artificial eye. He would later become Prime Minister and play a brief but important role on the domestic scene. He allotted to our organization a percentage of the income from the Iranian customs duties and a percentage of the income from gasoline sales. Later we would get permission to organize and administer a national lottery.

With this kind of financing, we were able to take our services into the provinces. In less than a year we had built 250 clinics in remote parts of the country. We did have some problems staffing these clinics at first, since Iran did not have many trained physicians, and those we had were not eager to work in these remote areas. We solved the problem by hiring doctors from other countries, mainly from India and Austria.

On the political front, however, we faced serious and more complex problems. While the Allied countries marked their war victories with national celebrations, Iran had little cause for rejoicing. We were still a poor country, our limited economy severely dislocated by the war, our administrative machinery a shambles.

According to the terms of the 1942 British and Russian alliance with Iran, the Allied forces were supposed to leave Iran six months after the war ended. But the Russians' wartime activities in Azerbaijan clearly showed they were not planning to evacuate this area, which they had coveted for so long. With the support of the Red Army, the Communist Tudeh party was reorganized in Azerbaijan and renamed the Democratic Party. Its armed members captured army and gendarmerie posts, and in December 1945 they proclaimed the "Autonomous Republic of Azerbaijan," under the leadership of Jafar Pishevari, a long-time Communist who had spent many years in Russia.

My brother dispatched troops from Teheran to recapture the province, but these were stopped by Russian tanks at Sharifabad, 150 kilometers out of Teheran. Encouraged by their success in Azerbaijan, the Communists, who had infiltrated the Kurdish tribes during the war, instigated another separatist revolt, which ended in the establishment of another so-called independent republic in Kurdistan in western Iran. This triggered even further separatist activity, this time by tribes in the south.

In Teheran another form of separatism prevailed. As I have mentioned before, there were so many shadings of political thinking in Parliament that no government could achieve a majority. It was a time of demonstrations in the streets, inflammatory newspaper articles.

Since the Communists represented the only disciplined political force in Teheran, the Prime Minister, Ahmad Qavam (Qavam Saltaneh), formed a cabinet which included three Tudeh ministers. At the same time, he established his own Democratic Party. Although Qavam was 70 years old, he was an extremely charismatic politician. An aristocrat through and through, Qavam was something of a martinet. He allowed no chairs in his office except his own, so that no one else, not even his own ministers, could sit in his presence. Nor would he allow members of Parliament to speak directly to him. Qavam insisted that remarks be addressed to his secretary, who in turn would relay the speech to "His Excellency." If anyone forgot this rule and spoke directly to the Prime Minister, he would turn to his secretary and ask, "What is this gentleman saying?"

While some of his personal poses were rather affected, Qavam was a political power to be reckoned with, and only a few months after the formation of his Democratic Party he felt confident enough to dismiss his Tudeh ministers. On the hundredth day of its existence, the Democratic Party took to the streets of Teheran, its members marching in their special uniforms, in an unusual show of solidarity. Some of my brother's friends and supporters warned him that Qavam's personal popularity and his growing power, if unchecked, could present problems for the monarchy, despite his demands for a more unified government.

It was over the issue of Azerbaijan, however, that my brother first became uneasy about Qavam's policies. The Shah had often told me that losing Azerbaijan would be like losing an arm, and that he meant to do everything within his power to regain the province. Early in 1946 Iran had lodged a formal protest before the UN Security Council against the armed Russian presence in Azerbaijan. (This was, incidentally, the first issue to come before that newly formed body.) Nevertheless, representatives of Qavam's government initiated negotiations with the representatives of the Communist "republic." I was completely against such talks, since I felt any negotiations would constitute a *de facto* recognition of this separatist regime. When, in February 1946, Qavam went to Russia to meet with Stalin, the Shah decided it was time to take some direct personal action.

Within the framework of my welfare activities, I had some contacts with the Russian hospital in Teheran, which was administered by a Russian-Armenian; on behalf of the Russian Red Cross, he arranged an invitation for me to visit Russia. It was, of course, understood that the Red Cross invitation was a cover, that even though I would be visiting hospitals, there would at some point be a meeting with Stalin and the opportunity for serious political discussion.

In April 1946 I left Teheran with a small staff which included a military adjutant, General Shafai, aboard a Russian airplane. At Moscow Airport we were greeted by the President of the Ukrainian Republic and several ministers who accompanied us to the quarters reserved for high-ranking foreign visitors. The following day I was asked to approve the official agenda for my trip, which was to include visits to Kiev, Kharkov, Leningrad, and Stalingrad.

In the years since, I have made many trips to Russia, but the details of that first visit still seem vivid. This Russia, this vast, wild country to the north, was at the same time our close neighbor and a great power to be feared. But now it was a wounded giant, visibly scarred from the war, which had left its mark everywhere.

On the outskirts of Leningrad I saw the remains of hundreds and hundreds of German tanks and cannons, the silent gray ghosts of a war machine that had died. I visited the Hermitage (which has an extensive Iranian collection), the cities, and the historical landmarks; everywhere there were souvenirs of the war. In the cities I saw chain gangs, young men in ragged clothes doing heavy construction work, moving rubble, laying bricks, repairing foundations. When I asked about these work crews, I was told that they were German prisoners of war who had been assigned the task of rebuilding what their army had destroyed. I was anxious to talk to these young men, to find out where they came from and what they knew of their families and children, but my military adjutant said it would be unwise to bring up the question.

Stalingrad was almost a ruin, with only the strongest and most massive buildings still standing. Only the Volga was unaffected by war, as it flowed wide and peaceful toward the Caspian Sea.

We were given accommodations in a military barracks decorated with pictures of the Stalingrad campaign, for it was at this spot that the German Sixth Army, commanded by Field-Marshal Paulus, was surrounded and defeated, an event that marked the turning point in the war between Russia and Germany.

Our Russian hosts were extremely hospitable and gracious, but no one was willing to discuss my projected meeting with Stalin. No mention of a meeting appeared on the official agenda, but I had been privately assured that the Generalissimo was ready to receive me. One afternoon at two o'clock my military adjutant came to see me, smiling broadly, with the news that we were going to see Stalin in an hour.

I've always thought of myself as a strong person, one who is able to maintain at least a surface calm and an air of assurance in the face of difficult or unpleasant situations. But now that I was actually on my way to meet the most powerful man in the Eastern hemisphere, a man with a reputation that was both awesome and frightening, my nerves were not as steady as I would have hoped. This meeting was much more important than the usual state visit, and I still didn't know exactly what I would say to this man who controlled the destiny of a vital portion of my country. As we were driving to the Kremlin, I checked my appearance in a small hand mirror, which then slipped from my hands and shattered into a dozen fragments. I am superstitious, and my apprehension about meeting Stalin was heightened by what I took to be a bad omen.

When I arrived at the Kremlin, accompanied by General Shafai, my adjutant, a Russian interpreter, and my lady-in-waiting, we were saluted by a young officer, who said something in Russian to the interpreter. I was informed that from this point on I would have to proceed alone. The Russian translator and I climbed several flights of stairs, walked through long corridors, crossing huge reception halls as we passed. Everywhere I saw massive crystal chandeliers, magnificent paintings, and other valuable *objets d'art*. At last we reached a great, rectangular hall dominated by many ornamental chandeliers and a baronial red carpet in the center of the floor. Arranged around the carpet, almost like decorative toy soldiers, were uniformed guards carrying ornamental spears. We were joined in this hall by the Chief of Protocol, who then proceeded to walk a few steps ahead of us as we made our way through yet another of these endless halls. I had never before visited anyone under such formal conditions, and I found the absolute silence and solemnity both ironic and intriguing. I had somehow imagined that the state atmosphere of a Communist country, especially after a great war, would somehow be more— I don't know, proletarian, perhaps. But here I was, in the midst of a pomp and circumstance I would have associated with the imperial tsars.

We came to a monumental door which took us into still another reception room, where five Russian officers, all heavily decorated with medals and other military ornaments, stood rigidly at attention. One of these officers pointed to a chair, and since he seemed to be inviting me to sit down, I did. All of these rituals had unsettled me even more, and I couldn't imagine what might be coming next. Considering the state of affairs between our two nations, I had a hard time pushing aside a recurring fantasy that somehow I might be arrested and sent to the famous Lubyanka prison, never to be heard from again.

The ring of a telephone interrupted my fantasy. One of the officers answered the call, and after a brief exchange he signaled me to walk toward another set of massive doors on the far end of the room. These doors were manned by two civilian servants, who showed me into another large room. For a moment I thought the room was empty, that it was just another way station in this complicated journey. I was startled when I caught a glimpse of someone standing at the far end of the room. I took a few steps forward—and realized I was in the presence of Generalissimo Josef Stalin.

He was not at all what I had expected. I had imagined someone as big and terrifying as his reputation, but here was a short, rather soft, plump man with broad shoulders and a thick mustache. He might have been a coachman or a doorman—except for his eyes, which were dark and piercing and, yes, frightening.

The first thing he did was to stretch out his hands in a gesture of welcome and then take my hand, shaking it vigorously. He led me to a couch, where we sat facing each other, and he started speaking (an interpreter seated behind him) in a low, monotonous voice, scarcely moving his lips.

I think he must have noticed that I was tense, because he began with some small talk, friendly, innocuous remarks that were meant to put me at ease. I had been told by the Chief of Protocol that our meeting would last for only ten minutes, since the Generalissimo had many other engagements. But Stalin did not seem to be in a great hurry, and when the Chief of Protocol came in to whisper something in his ear, Stalin waved him away.

I didn't know how much time I would have, so I took a deep breath and started to talk, and the essentials of what I said I can now reveal here. I reminded the Generalissimo that after the revolution Lenin had cancelled all the imperialistic benefits the Tsar had enjoyed in Iran, thus gaining the respect and admiration of our people. I pleaded as passionately as I could for an end to Russian support for the Azerbaijan "Republic," trying to convince Stalin that this puppet state would strain relations between our two countries for years to come. In the long run, I added, Iran's friendship and trust would be more valuable to the Soviet Union, since we were willing to cooperate in the development of economic ties with our northern neighbor. Stalin listened attentively, not interrupting, and sending away the Chief of Protocol each time he tried to say something about ending our meeting. By this time we had been talking for more than an hour.

When I stopped talking, Stalin began to build gradually on the theme that Iran would not need "other friends" in addition to the Soviet Union. He made several oblique references to our complaint to the UN, arguing that disputes between our countries should be resolved through mutual understanding and negotiations, without the interference of any foreign force or organization. He warned me that Iran should not try to oppose Russia on the basis of support from the Americans. In Stalin's mind, it was he who had defeated the Axis powers, and he made it clear he was not afraid of America and Great Britain.

As he spoke, I formed a picture of a man who was not a Communist intellectual by any means, but rather a pragmatic realist who ruled Russia in an almost imperial manner. Although he was willing to use armed force whenever he thought it was useful, he knew full well his country could not afford any large-scale conflict, but he made his political choices based on the certainty that no one else could afford such conflicts either.

At the time of our talk, I believe he had already come to the conclusion that a Communist revolution in Iran was not a viable prospect. So he pressed instead for some realistic gains, specifically for the establishment of a joint Soviet-Iranian oil venture for the exploitation of oil in Azerbaijan.

He brought up the subject of the Russian-Iranian oil agreement that had been drafted by Prime Minister Qavam and by the Soviet Ambassador Sadchukov, I tried to remain noncommital, listening to what he had to say, neither agreeing nor disagreeing. This seemed to satisfy him, so before our discussion ended, I expressed the hope that Russia would stop its "cold war" activities in Iran (the Soviets first employed these techniques in Iran, before the phrase "cold war" had been coined).

Our ten-minute meeting had lasted for two and a half hours, and when it was over Stalin offered me his hand and escorted me to the door. Before I left, he put his hand on my shoulder, looked into my eyes, and said: "Give my best regards to your brother, the Shahanshah, and tell him that if he had ten like you, he would have no worries at all." Turning to the interpreter, and pointing to me, he said: "*Ana Pravda Patriot* [Here is a true patriot]."

The following day I was scheduled to visit a Moscow hospital, but I was informed that the trip had been cancelled. Instead I was invited by Generalissimo Stalin to join him for a sport ceremony at Moscow's largest stadium. When I arrived at the stadium, I was taken to Stalin's box, and the Generalissimo gallantly offered me the seat next to his. Several high-ranking Soviet officials were already seated, including Mr. Molotov, who was readily recognizable by his round spectacles and his distinctive Mongol face. Once the formal introductions were made, I sat back, ready to relax and enjoy the program of athletic and folk events.

Now that our political "business" had been concluded, Stalin became a gracious, attentive host. Before I meet with a public figure, I always try to do my homework, reading whatever biographical information I can find. In Stalin's case, I knew that he had never received a princess, nor did he have any fondness for any monarchic regime. But on a personal level he was most solicitous that day, looked at me often, asked if I was comfortable, offered me tea and cakes, and told me a little bit about each of the events we were watching.

Before I left Russia, Stalin sent me a magnificent sable coat. This gift made some rather splashy headlines, but I still cherish it as the souvenir of my first mission in foreign diplomacy.

As I could have predicted after my discussion with Stalin, Ambassador Sadchukov continued to press for ratification of the Qavam-Sadchukov agreement and for the creation of the Irano-Soviet Oil Company. Yet even though such a joint venture seemed to be in the offing, Iran did not withdraw its complaint from the UN, despite extreme pressure from the Russians. In this we had the support of the United States and other Western powers, for by now the wartime "marriage of convenience" between East and West was in serious trouble and the cold war had officially begun. President Truman would no longer ignore the nature of Russian activity in Iran and Turkey.

UN debates on this activity reached a peak in the spring of 1946, with the Soviets constantly threatening to withdraw from the Security Council. But on the issue of Azerbaijan, the Russians backed down and evacuated their troops, apparently willing for the moment to be content with an oil agreement.

The Red Army withdrew, and seven months later, Iranian troops, personally commanded by the Shah, attacked Azerbaijan from three fronts. Deprived of its military support, the puppet republic quickly collapsed, and on December 10, 1946, the Shah's troops entered Tabriz, where they were cheered by the population.

A week later the Shah's army took Mahabad, in Kurdistan, thus ending the one-year existence of both Russian-sponsored separatist "republics." In October 1947 the Qavam-Sadchukov oil agreement was brought before the Iranian Parliament, which voted 102 to 2 against it. In doing so, the members referred to a 1944 law (initiated by a parliamentary deputy who would soon become world-famous, Dr. Mohammed Mossadegh) which forbade the government to negotiate any oil agreement with a foreign power without the prior consent of the Parliament.

With the resolution of the Azerbaijan issue, which the people of Iran saw as a major national victory, my brother's personal popularity soared, and during his first visit to the newly liberated province he was greeted by huge mobs of cheering people.

Yet the Shah's political power was still not very secure, and there were those who felt that a strong and ambitious prime minister, like Ahmad Qavam, could pose a serious threat to the monarchy. Through his Democratic Party, Qavam had moved swiftly to consolidate and strengthen his personal power, which he used to maintain a tight grip on the reins of government.

In July 1947 the parliamentary elections resulted in a clear majority for the followers of Ahmad Qavam, who was once again appointed Prime Minister. Speculation increased among the foreign diplomatic community, and within some

Iranian political circles, that Qavam could, if he chose, overthrow the Shah.

Although Qavam was an old-fashioned politician who believed that women had no place in politics, he did talk to me from time to time and had, on several occasions, even asked my advice. One evening, in December 1947, I invited Qavam to come to my house, and without mincing any words, I told him what I had heard about his political ambitions.

He did not seem surprised, but he looked at me steadily and said: "These allegations are completely false. I have always been loyal to the monarchy." Sensing that I still doubted him, he went on: "What would the Princess have me do to prove that I would never jeopardize the monarchy?"

I looked through his dark glasses, into his eyes, and said calmly; "The best proof of your loyalty would be your resignation."

He reacted as if I had struck him. Obviously shaken, he answered: "I have no intention of resigning, and no power on earth can make me do so against my will. Tomorrow I will arrange to get a vote of confidence from the Parliament."

The following day he asked for an extraordinary session of Parliament, at which he requested a vote of confidence. To his dismay, Qavam could not get a majority and was forced to resign.

Actually, I had not been bluffing: through my contacts with various members of Parliament, I knew they would not give Qavam a vote of confidence should he ask for one. A few years later I would have a similar confrontation with another prime minister, Dr. Mohammed Mossadegh, but this time there would be a much different outcome.

Before World War II, Iran's cultural contacts with other countries had been extremely limited. Before my father's day, wealthy families often sent their children to Russia for an education, and later to Germany or France. Some aristocratic families made occasional visits to the resorts and major cities of Europe, but for the most part the people of Iran and the people of the West were unknown quantities to each other. (Now, after decades of contact in an ever-shrinking world, I fear that this is still, unhappily, true.)

To most Americans, Iran did not even exist. So it can be said that after World War II our two countries were just beginning to make serious contact, without a shared history of either trusted friendship or of past mistakes and re-criminations. America came to Iran with relatively clean hands that were extended in a giving rather than a taking position. But in their innocence, the Americans brought with them a naiveté that often bordered on arrogance, an assump-tion that because America is one of the most powerful nations in the world, it has the best way of life. From this assumption, it was logical to assume that Asian and African countries were economically underdeveloped because their cultures were somehow "backward" or "inferior." Out of this kind of reasoning, Americans evolved a rather original way of helping other cultures, namely by trying to make them as "American" as possible.

In saying this, I don't mean to belittle America's good intentions, but rather to suggest that help without under-standing can create problems for the giver as well as the recipient. Take, for example, the Point Four Program, which was established after the war to administer U.S. aid to Iran and other countries and to provide technical assistance.

The administrative and bureaucratic procedures of Point Four personnel made an enormous impression on Iran. Let me explain first that the atmosphere in Iranian offices was fairly formal. Although almost none of our office buildings were air-conditioned at that time, no employee would take his jacket off, not even in the heat of summer. No more would he sit on his desk or put his feet up on it.

A visitor to any office would be offered tea while his

host listened politely to whatever proposition was being presented. The word "no" would almost never be heard in business discussions, and even if there was no interest at all in the subject under discussion, courtesy required the use of gentle words and techniques to discourage the unwanted visitor. As the reader might guess, this was only part of a very leisurely way of doing business: a milieu in which deadlines were flexible, lunch hours were equally flexible, and occupational ulcers were virtually unheard of.

Needless to say, the Americans were appalled by this "inefficiency" and quickly set out to indoctrinate Iranian employees in the "American way" of doing things. Some of the results were quite unexpected. Our people picked up American mannerisms very quickly: they learned how to dress more casually for work, how to lounge around their offices, how to slap fellow employees on the back and address their superiors in familiar terms. They even learned how to say "no"—without first offering a cup of tea. But they did not—could not—become efficient by Western standards simply by adopting the superficial manifestations of behavior that was completely alien to them.

When the Point Four administrators did hire Iranian personnel, it was at salaries that were closer to American standards than to prevailing local salaries. This created enormous disparities between Iranians who worked for the Americans and Iranians who worked for private business or for their own government. A secretary employed by Point Four, for example, might earn as much as a top manager in other organizations. While those inflated salaries were undoubtedly a blessing to the few who earned them, this kind of disregard for local conditions (which was by no means confined to Iran) generated feelings of frustration, wonder, envy, admiration, and resentment—all the ingredients, in fact, that are part of the relationship between a "have" and a "have not," whether individuals or nations.

Unquestionably the Point Four specialists helped our country solve several chronic, serious problems. For example, the program's agricultural and public health experts traveled to the remotest regions of the country to implement various pest-control strategies which resulted in the virtual elimination of such traditional plagues as grasshoppers and malaria-carrying mosquitoes.

If efforts like this were sublime, some were also ridiculous. Point Four's animal husbandry specialists apparently took careful note of the fact that Iranian donkeys tended to be rather small. To correct this "problem" (given the American penchant for "bigger is better" thinking, I suppose small donkeys might seem like one of Nature's mistakes), the program imported by airplane, at enormous cost, large donkeys from Cyprus to cross with our small ones. In a country that had so many real and urgent needs, the "new improved" breed of donkeys became something of a local joke, one that would cause our people to shake their heads in bafflement and wonder at the strange priorities of the Americans.

Another organization that promoted Iranian-American contact after the war was the United States Information Service (USIS), which arranged exchange programs whereby our journalists could visit America. Upon their return, they invariably wrote long, breathless articles describing in minute detail every exotic wonder of the New World. The newspapers publishing those articles, which told us about such phenomena as skyscrapers and "cafeterias" and "supermarkets," were much in demand. These stories captured the imaginations of our young people, who began to see the United States as a marvelous place to pursue a higher education. An American education offered another attractive benefit: the student who had one could return to Iran and immediately be hired by a Point Four program at a very handsome salary. Among the Iranians who followed such a course were Ardeshir Zahedi, who became the Iranian Ambassador to the United States.

I must confess that I was as intrigued as any young student by the opportunity to visit America; that came in August 1947, through an invitation by the Red Cross. I was met at the airport by a representative of the Mayor of New York; our Ambassador to the United States, Hossein Ala; and representatives from the State Department and the Red Cross.

Now that I have spent so much time in New York (at least part of each year for over a decade) I don't always notice the texture and detail of this extraordinary city. But that first look at Manhattan's skyscrapers shimmering in the midday sun, the teeming throngs of people moving so purposefully and quickly through the streets, accompanied by the insistent discords of city noises—this was a first impression to remember forever.

Our Ambassador had arranged acccommodations in the Waldorf Towers, but I didn't want to waste any time resting or getting settled. I set out immediately to explore the city. I soon realized that New York was not like Paris or the Swiss cities, where you could stroll at a leisurely pace for hours. New York was a diverse city, sometimes beautiful, sometimes grim, sometimes aggressively functional, but always exciting and dynamic.

The first thing that struck me about the American way of life was the abundance of food. I had come from a country where food was still scarce, and even in London, where I had stopped on my way to America, many foods were rationed and an egg for breakfast was a luxury even in the finest hotels. I couldn't believe the quantities of food Americans threw away because they weren't "fresh enough," until I realized that America had not been touched by the war in the same ways as the rest of the world.

The enormous variety of consumer goods in postwar America also amazed me. Apparently one could walk into an automobile showroom and buy a car, an impossibility in Iran or in most of Europe. Or one could choose from hundreds of shoes, clothing items, and labor-saving devices. America was like a huge bazaar that not even Aladdin's genie could have conjured up.

During my two weeks in New York I behaved like a typical tourist. I saw my first rodeo in Madison Square Garden and my first American parade. There was a convention of war veterans in the city at the time, and thousands of them marched on Fifth Avenue, cheered by the civilian crowds, who showered them with multicolored confetti.

I visited museums and art galleries, and I spent hours listening to radio programs which featured guests like Bob Hope, Bing Crosby, James Stewart, Abbott and Costello, and Laurel and Hardy—names I knew from movies I had seen.

I've never been overly concerned with clothes, but before prices climbed so high, I used to buy a few new things each year from European designers like Lanvin or Dior (nowadays I patronize the boutiques that carry the *prêt à porter* designs of these houses). During my New York visit I saw the first wave of the "New Look" in store windows and on the city's fashionable women. I thought this heavily structured look, with all its pads and laces and yards of fabric was not especially flattering to American women, who had such naturally attractive figures.

Since I was scheduled to meet President Truman after my New York trip, I decided to buy a new dress—an American dress—for the occasion. One of the women who had come to the United States with me told me she had heard about a fashion show at Saks Fifth Avenue, conducted by Sophie Gimbel, and that is where I had my introduction to American style in clothes.

After the experiences of my Russian visit, I found Washington quite startling. The Kremlin was the seat of a Communist government of a war-torn country, but everything there spoke of aristocracy, opulence, and formality. The White House, on the other hand, was the official residence of the President of the wealthiest capitalist country in the world, but it was simple, unpretentious, and relaxed. President Truman and his wife Bess reinforced this feeling of honest simplicity, for they both had the easy informality of "people next door."

I liked Harry Truman at once. Although the press occasionally poked fun at his bluntness and his supposed lack of polish, I found his decisive, straightforward manner very refreshing. Talking to him did not require any kind of diplomatic games, and he seemed very much aware of Iran's most pressing problems.

He asked me about my meeting with Stalin, but before I could answer, he said: "I am pretty darned tired of baby-sitting those Russians. . . . We warned them when they were in Azerbaijan, and now we've had to warn them again to keep their hands off Greece." He added that he hoped the Greeks would follow the Iranian example and defend their country against Communist infiltration.

The cold war activities of the Soviets were, understandably, the dominant topic of conversation. Earlier that same week a group of Greek Communist guerillas under the leadership of General Marcus Vafiades had proclaimed the establishment of an independent state in northern Greece. The Athens government had called this movement the "act two" of the aborted takeover in Azerbaijan, warning the Russians to expect the same results. General Dwight D. Eisenhower, who was then the American Chief of Staff, had said the United States would not allow Greece to become "a vassal of Russia," and the talk around Washington was that U.S. troops might be sent into Greece.

I assured President Truman that Iran would always be a good friend to the United States, that my brother was committed to the building of a modern and independent nation. We concluded our visit on a very friendly note, with a round of invitations on both sides. I told the Trumans that President Roosevelt had expressed a wish to see Iran in peacetime (he had not lived to make the trip), and I invited them to visit Teheran at their earliest convenience. President Truman expressed the hope that the Shah would visit America soon—my brother did make the trip in 1948, when he met with the President and Dean Acheson—and Bess Truman urged me to return to Washington to "see the 'new' White House after we finish our restoration project."

While I was in Washington, I gave a large party at our Embassy so I could get to know American officials, elected representatives, and journalists. I remember *Time* magazine's comments on these events which appeared in the issue of September 8, 1947: "In Washington last week a slender, dark girl saw with her own eyes that Persia had powerful friends in the U.S. Several hundred people thronged the elegant red brick Persian Embassy to shake hands with Her Imperial Highness Ashraf Pahlevi [sic], twin sister of Persia's ruling Shah. President Truman received her in the White House, and Bess Truman was there too. This week the State Department scheduled a big, brilliant reception."

It was a reception hosted by Secretary of State George Marshall, founder of the Marshall Plan, which gave economic aid to Europe for postwar reconstruction. As the architect of this American program, Marshall had come under heavy attack by the Soviet bloc countries; Anna Pauker, Secretary-General of the Rumanian Communist Party, had called him a fascist. When I talked with Marshall, I found him to be a sophisticated, intelligent, and humane man, genuinely dedicated to the fight against poverty and hunger; the Nobel Prize he won in 1953 was well deserved. Marshall was, of course, keenly aware of the global strategies of the cold war, and although he told me that his Plan was not directed against any country or doctrine, he was obviously not prepared to extend any assistance to those nations who were part of the hostile and noncooperating Soviet bloc. For example, he warned any nations not participating in the Paris Conference (which was called to discuss the procedures and implementations of his program) not to expect any U.S. aid, and he did cut off assistance to Romania, Poland, and Hungary.

Since Iran was one of the main targets of the Soviet cold war strategies (the Russians were still trying to pressure the Parliament into approving the establishment of the Irano-Russian Oil Company), I was very relieved to meet politicians like Truman and Marshall, men who understood the nature of Russian intrigues in Iran and the kind of problems these created for us.

In the years that followed I would meet other American presidents, but after Truman, it seemed on the whole that Republican presidents were more sympathetic than their Democratic counterparts to the problems of Iran. I don't know whether this is because Republican politicans were more comfortable with the concept of a monarchy, the result of their traditionally more conservative philosophies, or whether it has been more a question of individual personalities.

One American quality that seems to cut across party lines, at least one that has become significantly more pronounced since the Vietnam conflict, is a strong tendency toward a return to isolationism. Although the United States has participated in two world wars, has accepted more than its share of economic responsibilities to the less fortunate nations of the world, has actively cooperated in the establishment of the United Nations, American politicans seem reluctant now to accept the full implications of superpower status. Obviously domestic affairs provide the issues that make or break American political careers, and unless there exists a direct military threat to American security, it is a rare president, secretary of state, senator, or congressman who will risk the wrath of the American electorate these days by advocating American involvement in global politics in any well-coordinated, long-term policy where there is a risk of military confrontation. In this, they reflect the thinking of the American electorate who believe that the United States has no business meddling further in the Middle East, Latin America, Africa, or Asia. Ironically this sentiment intensified during a period of time when the world shrank to only two "neighbors" —the so-called "free world" and the Soviet satellite countries. Back in the days when Theodore Roosevelt advocated walking softly but carrying a big stick, America could perhaps afford lapses into isolationism; but now, when Roosevelt's advice would make excellent sense, there is a growing suspicion, among America's friends as well as her enemies, that whether America speaks softly or harshly, the American public will not allow any administration to wield any stick at all. This may explain, in part, why we have the spectacle of America being openly mocked—in Iran and elsewhere—by demagogues who are confident that the United States will suffer almost any indignity, provided it is committed on foreign soil, and respond with nothing more than empty threats.

While a government such as that of the United States must clearly be responsive to the wishes of its people, it must create and implement an effective and consistent foreign policy, and I do not think it has done that as far as Iran is concerned. The alternative is a future in which events like those in Teheran and Afghanistan will be repeated elsewhere, and a future in which the kind of confrontations that Americans dread most will materialize with alarming frequency.

Although the memories of Vietnam have dictated a foreign policy that is passive and reactive, rather than one that is active and dynamic, the failures in Vietnam do not alone explain why America has found itself "held hostage" by a country infinitely weaker than itself, why its embassies abroad are besieged and burned, and why it is the universal

99

"enemy" in the so-called Islamic revival throughout the Middle East.

These events are the results of failures of perception, of understanding—of education about the most basic elements of the Middle Eastern world—which are decades old. When I first came to America in 1947, Iran had been the focus of the first major East-West confrontation, the subject of intense UN debates, and all of these events presumably were reported in the American press. I found that many Americans did not even know that a country named Iran existed, let alone what it was like. Even among the diplomatic corps and among well-educated people, there was a vagueness about who the Iranians were or what the culture was, a tendency to confuse Iran with Iraq or to mistakenly assume that Iran is an Arab country simply because it is an Islamic nation. This fuzziness about the world outside is unique to America; among the intelligentsia of the European countries, for example, there is generally a higher level of awareness and information regarding cultures other than their own.

Today every citizen in every city and town in America unquestionably knows that Iran exists. But what else does he know? He understands that for the time being there will be no more Iranian oil, that this may directly affect his life with rising prices and more fuel shortages. But I think when he turns on his television set and sees angry Iranian mobs and hears elaborate rhetorical denunciations of the United States, his understanding of Iranian psychology and politics is probably not much greater than it would have been a generation ago. Nor do most media accounts add to his fund of information. Aside from an occasional cogent and thoughtful historical and sociological analysis, much of what appears in print is distorted (not to mention inaccurate), reducing broad social and political issues to their simplest dimensions.

Since so many of today's stories refer, albeit fleetingly, to Iran's crisis years of the early 1950's, a period during which the Shah almost lost his throne, it would seem that a better understanding of present events can be gained from a reexamination of those early years. It may come as a surprise to many, I think, but there are startling similarities between the events and personalities of that 1950's period and the characters and conditions one sees on television today. These similarities demonstrate the turbulent and cyclical nature of Iranian politics and the disruptive forces (both internal and external) which my brother had to face throughout his reign. Had America better understood those events, it might have learned more about the fundamental nature of Iran and therefore avoided the crisis that the world witnesses today.

The dominant theme of the 1950's was oil. This precious and volatile substance which we call *naft* was believed by the ancient Persians to be a divine symbol of life. In their religious "fire temples," the ancients incorporated the "fire altars," a natural phenomenon created by the spontaneous burning of oil which had seeped to the earth's surface.

The modern history of our Iranian oil begins in 1872, when Baron Julius de Reuter (a naturalized British subject) was granted a sweeping concession which included the right to exploit the mineral deposits (including oil) in western Persia. Under a more limited concession issued in 1889, De Reuter formed the Persian Bank Mining Rights Corporation, which explored unsuccessfully for a number of years until 1901, when the firm was dissolved.

Although no oil was found in the west during these initial explorations, the governor of the western province of Kermanshah continued to believe that it existed. At his request, the French archaeologist Jacques de Morgan conducted a systematic study of Persia's petroleum resources. De Morgan's research, which was published in Europe, attracted the attention of William Knox D'Arcy, an Englishman who had already made a considerable fortune in Australian gold mines. In 1901 D'Arcy acquired a concession for the exploitation of oil in southern Iran. Under the terms of this concession, which was to last for 60 years, D'Arcy was to pay the Persian government 20,000 pounds, 20,000 shares in his company, and 16 percent of his net profits. The British government, which realized the importance of D'Arcy's concession, acquired the majority of shares in his company in May of 1914.

The first oil explorations in southern Iran (Khuzestan) were carried out under extremely harsh conditions. Daytime temperatures reached 130 degrees Fahrenheit, clean drinking water was limited, and sanitary facilities were practically nonexistent. The problems of the pioneer oil workers and engineers were compounded by the local tribes, which occasionally raided the oil camps and carried off moveable equipment and personal property.

To protect the lives and properties of the oil personnel, Britain sent a company of Indian soldiers into southern Persia. Although this was a clear violation of Persian sovereignty, the Qajar king lacked the power (and perhaps even the inclination) to make a formal protest. The only step the king did take to protect his own interest in D'Arcy's venture was to appoint a retired customs official as his personal representative at the oil company's local headquarters. This official's role was immediately neutralized—on the first day of his employment, in fact—when he was placed on the company's confidential payroll. Obviously he was thereafter more concerned with the company's interests than with the interests of Iran. Here I must comment on the kind of deal-making that would taint a great many transactions with foreigners, not only in Iran, but throughout the Middle East.

The tradition of *baksheesh*, of payment for favors or services rendered, is an old one. Intrinsically the concept of *baksheesh* is no more dishonorable than the idea of a *pourboire* or tip. As is the case in the West, however, *baksheesh* came to be used in Iran in various bureaucratic transactions: to expedite the processing of an official form, to facilitate the passage of a shipment through customs, and so on. But in the 1950's, as I saw Iran becoming increasingly interesting to foreign firms, for investment, for large-scale development schemes, for enormously lucrative sales, I saw the escalation of *baksheesh* into some fairly sophisticated pay-off techniques, all designed to give one foreign firm or government some kind of advantage over another. While my brother certainly did not condone these practices (indeed he periodically waged serious campaigns to eliminate corruption in the Iranian bureaucracy), he saw a certain irony in the fact that Iranian corruption was most heartily condemned in the Western press, the press of those very countries most actively involved in promoting large-scale sales or enormously profitable business ventures at whatever cost, that is, "by hook or by crook."

Clearly the Iranian oil industry, with its enormous profit potential, would from the beginning offer considerable possibilities not only for the exercise of doubtful business practices but also for a rather lopsided distribution of these profits. In the beginning, however, the Persian government had no choice but to allow foreigners to exploit Persian oil on whatever terms they offered. Obviously, in the early years of the twentieth century Persia did not have the money and technology to develop its own oil resources or the political power to negotiate equitable arrangements. In time, conditions would change and Iran would demand more of a share in its own resources and more of a voice in their management.

But in those early years of oil exploration, there were virtually no profits to discuss or distribute. In the first two years of D'Arcy's venture, some 250,000 pounds were spent without producing a single drop of oil. In January 1904, D'Arcy's troubles seemed to be over when one of his wells struck oil, but after a few months the well ran dry, and the company's finances were in critical condition. To keep his operation solvent, D'Arcy merged with Burmah Oil, which had previously been active in southeast Asia. Finally, on May 26, 1908, after years of nothing but grueling work and dry wells, the first gusher was brought in, at Masjid-i-Sulaiman, about 150 miles north of Abadan. This discovery marked the beginning of the oil industry, not only in Iran, but in the entire Middle East.

Now that oil had actually been found, the problem of protecting natural interest came up again. This was a period when the Teheran government had no power at all, and when the tribal chieftains were the principal arbiters of law and order; in some ways, conditions resembled those of the American "wild west" of a century before. The drillers had been paying "protection money" to the Bakhtiari chieftains, but now it was necessary to make an arrangement whereby these chieftains would receive a share of oil revenues. Before a pipeline and a refinery could be built, it was also necessary to make a financial arrangement with the Shaikh Khazal of Muhammara, whose personal control extended to Abadan Island and the area surrounding the port of Khorramshahr. Once these arrangements had been completed, the oil syndicate formed the Anglo-Persian Oil Company, which was later known as the Anglo-Iranian Oil Company and in 1954 became the British Petroleum Company (BP).

The pipeline from Masjid-i-Sulaiman to Abadan was completed by 1912, and during the first full year of production (1913), Persia produced 80,000 tons of petroleum; within five years the figures increased more than threefold.

It was clear that Persia's oil industry would be a substantial one, but as yet the country was not itself realizing any great benefits from this industry. Even before he became Shah, my father was concerned, on a military level, with bringing the oil-producing areas under the control of the Teheran government, such as it was at the time. One by one, he had subdued the major tribes—the Lurs, the Qashqai, the Kurds, and ultimately the Bakhtiari (in spite of a strong British protest against any interference with the chieftains they considered their friends). When, in 1924, my father began a campaign to end the autonomous regime of the Shaikh of Muhammara, the British lodged an even stronger protest. Ignoring this protest (the British would remember Reza Khan's uncompromising stance when they invaded Iran during World War II), my father took troops into the south and, in a bloodless military operation, ended the reign of the dissident shaikh, who was brought back to Teheran.

After he became Shah, my father began to familiarize himself with the workings of our oil industry. He saw at once that oil policy was completely dictated by company interests (which were, of course, identical with British interests), without any consideration for Persian needs.

On more than one occasion my father informed the company that he was dissatisfied with Iran's royalty percentages, with the scope of the original D'Arcy agreement, with the fact that no effort was being made to train Persian employees in the technical functions of oil production. A generation later the entire question of "technology transfer" would become a vital one in relations between technology-rich countries and those in various developmental stages.

When no new agreement could be reached by negotiations, Reza Shah cancelled the D'Arcy concession in 1932, a move that was approved by the Parliament and widely applauded by the Persian people. The British government was outraged (another mark against Reza Shah) and immediately submitted a formal protest to the League of Nations. The dispute was eventually resolved through direct negotiation between my father's government and the oil company. In a new agreement signed in 1933, Persia obtained somewhat better terms, including a royalty increase to 20 percent of net profits, a payment of four shillings on every ton of oil sold, a reduction of the concession area, and a promise that the company would "Persianize" the staff.

This 1933 agreement was the one still in effect in 1950. At this point the Abadan refinery, with a capacity of 500,000 barrels per day, was the largest in the world, and Iran's daily production was 700,000 barrels per day. Clearly Iran had become a major figure in the overall picture of world oil; nevertheless, we were still receiving a very small share in the exploitation of this major resource.

During this 17-year period, Anglo-Iranian Oil attempted to maintain its position without yielding any of its prerogatives, in spite of the fact that there was among the underdeveloped oil-producing countries of the world a new militancy vis-à-vis the oil companies. In 1938, for example, the Mexican government expropriated British and American oil properties. In Saudi Arabia, ARAMCO agreed to a 50–50 agreement in 1950, and in Venezuela, Standard Oil instructed its executives to "become a part of the country instead of remaining the representatives of an aloof foreign interest."

For the oil companies there were signposts all over the world, clear indicators that changes would have to come, in policies, in philosophies, and in techniques of doing business within their host countries. But as far as Anglo-Iranian Oil was concerned, there was no reason to change anything, in spite of a growing Iranian resentment against foreign intervention and exploitation.

It was at this crucial time in the history of Iranian oil that a Machiavellian genius emerged: an intellectual, a fanatic, a demagogue, a charismatic orator, and above all, a consummate showman. That man, who would wave the banner of "oil for Iranians," was Dr. Mohammed Mossadegh. He was a man who would declare war on the oil company and almost succeed in toppling the Shah. Even now, more than a decade after his death, it is difficult to describe to anyone who did not know him the phenomenon that was Mossadegh. He rallied enough support from diverse factions to become, for a time at least, the most powerful leader in Iran, and he created a period of economic and political crisis very similar to what we are seeing in Iran today.

Dr. Mossadegh was the son of a Qajar princess and a wealthy aristocrat who had been Minister of Finance under the Qajar king Ahmad Shah. After completing his studies in Switzerland and France, he returned to Iran and in 1915 began a career in politics as a member of Parliament. As a descendant of the Qajars, Mossadegh opposed my father's regime from the beginning, and early in Reza Shah's reign he was arrested on charges of plotting against the king. His health, which had never been very strong, began to fail in prison, and my brother interceded with my father for Mossadegh's release. This was one of the few instances I can remember when my brother disagreed with my father's decision. Mossadegh later made many public declarations of gratitude to my brother, but behind those declarations there was an implacable and undying enmity for the Pahlavis.

During the early years of World War II Mossadegh's political activities ceased, but in 1944 he was once again elected to Parliament. One of his early political successes was the passage that year of a bill prohibiting the government from entering into any oil agreements with foreign powers without the prior consent of the Parliament; it was on the basis of this law that Parliament voided the Sadchukov-Qavam oil agreement in 1947.

In the years following World War II Mossadegh was able to build considerable personal popularity and support, partly by mobilizing the anti-foreign sentiments that followed the Allied occupation. With eight other deputies, he founded the National Front, and with them he was able within a matter of months to control the Iranian Parliament.

While Mossadegh's rise to power may have seemed incredible by Western standards, his career has had similar counterparts in Iranian politics and indeed throughout the Middle East, particularly during periods of national uncertainty and confusion (even the United States during the cold war, anti-Communist period was not immune to the demagoguery and fanaticism of a man like Joseph McCarthy).

107

It is the hallmark of a politician like Mossadegh (or like Khomeini) that he can mobilize the masses by skillful manipulation of very basic, usually negative, emotions. It is also true that such politicians often have relatively brief periods of power because they collect a diversity of political opinion under a banner of extremes, under a banner that is "anti-this" or "anti-that." When the dust settles, when the emotionalism generated by their theatrical orchestration of such issues as the nationalization of oil or the taking of American hostages begins to die down, the support begins to fragment, and the original movement collapses or serves as a spearhead for another, well-planned, more sohisticated political program.

In Mossadegh's case, the anti-foreign note he sounded struck a chord in many Iranians, all the more so because his message was inspired by a genuine, albeit rather muddled, patriotism (which is quite different from the Khomeini's anti-American message). Mossadegh's rise to power came at a time when Iran was still the site of foreign intervention and interference. Our country was still poor and weak, our political system still vulnerable to various means of disruption and manipulation.

And, at that time, my brother reigned, but he still did not govern. Theoretically, he had the power to appoint the Prime Minister, but his choices were limited to politicians who could work effectively with, or around, the big powers—Russia, Britain, and America—whose goodwill was necessary to Iran's continued survival. Naturally, such politicians also had to have a broad base of political support in the Parliament, or at least the capacity to create such support on crucial issues. This was no easy task. For a Westerner who operates basically within a two- or three- or four-party system that has evolved through generations of movement and change, the Iranian Parliament of the 1940's and 1950's would have seemed like loosely organized chaos. For the Shah and several prime ministers, the Parliament could present the frustrating spectacle of political opinions almost as numerous as the deputies themselves.

According to our constitution then, a two-thirds quorum was required for conducting any business, and a three-fourths quorum was needed for voting on legislation. These rules, coupled with the multiplicity of political interests, made it an easy matter for small groups of individuals virtually to halt the legislative machinery merely by absenting themselves.

To the Westerner, this individualism and obstructionism might seem like part of the normal growing pains of a democratic system; but in fact they are not. The concept of a constitutional monarchy was, like so many of our modern institutions, not the product of our own culture, but rather the product of alien tradition, an imitation of something that we in the East had been indoctrinated to believe is stronger and more progressive and more serviceable.

Having imported the machinery of democracy to our shores, we faced the kind of acceptance-rejection forces that any transplant generates. We could conduct elections (like the Americans), go through the motions of parliamentary procedure (like the British), but in the minds of our people, and of many of our politicians, this was more *pro forma*, a "going through the motions," than it was a deeply felt belief and constructive use of government. The evolution of an Eastern-style democratic psychology would take time, and there would always be the possibility that this process might be interrupted or disrupted by outside intervention or internal crises.

During the postwar years such crisis and intervention were almost a daily fact of life. Take, for example, our system of elections. During that period, a candidate for Parliament had to have wealth or powerful connections in order to be elected. In the large cities it may have been possible for a man to be elected on the basis of his education, his personality, or his political ideas. But in the provinces, where the

masses of people were far removed intellectually and physically from what was happening in Teheran, votes were often
bought, with money or with influence, under conditions that
were similar to the operations of the old-time American
political machines. This meant that the successful parliamentary candidate was likely to be a wealthy landlord, a member
of an influential provincial family, or a man who had strong
connections among the clergy or with a foreign power (the
representatives of foreign powers often supplied money and
influence to support a candidate they favored). It wasn't
unusual for ballot boxes to be tampered with or for the
identity cards of deceased persons to be bought in bulk by
would-be parliamentary deputies (voting was done with
identity card).

It was in this political framework that my brother tried
to pick up the threads of my father's programs, to introduce
several of his own, and to maintain the delicate balance of
protecting Iran's sovereignty without antagonizing any major foreign power.

With these aims in mind, he appointed Abdolhossein
Hajir as Prime Minister in June 1948. Hajir was a good friend
of mine (and I must say I was to some extent instrumental in
his appointment) who had served previously as Minister of
Finance and Court Minister. Abdolhossein Hajir was an
intelligent, able, and loyal bureaucrat who could understand
and cope with the domestic and international issues. Yet this
appointment came under immediate attack by Ayatollah
Kashani, a cleric who had almost as much influence in his
time as Khomeini had at the time of the revolution. Ayatollah
Kashani had been born in Iraq and had fought in the
Ottoman army during the first World War. For his wartime
activity, he had been sentenced to death by the British, a
sentence he managed to escape by fleeing the country. From
then on he would bear a passionate hatred for the British and
for anyone he even suspected of dealing with them. Kashani
tried to come to Iran during Reza Shah's reign, but permis-

sion was refused. After my father's exile, he came to Teheran, where he proceeded to build a strong following among the "mafia" of the bazaar, the so-called *tchajho kesh* ("the drawers of knives"). These were the merchants of the fruit and vegetable market (Teheran's *Les Halles*), and with their support, Kashani could produce instant mobs to take a "pro" or an "anti" stance on almost any issue. (We see this today under Khomeini, where the regime seems to be able to mobilize mobs at will for the television cameras.)

Almost immediately after the Hajir appointment, Kashani organized demonstrations (during which a number of people were killed) attacking the new Prime Minister as an agent of the British government and as a British spy.

In the spring of 1950 Hajir was stabbed as he was entering a Teheran mosque. As soon as I heard about the incident, I rushed to the hospital, where I was met by two physicians who told me that there was nothing they could do to save him.

When I saw my friend, he was deathly pale and barely conscious. I touched his arm gently. "Mr. Hajir... it's Ashraf."

He opened his eyes with difficulty and tried to get up, but I put my hand on his forehead and told him to rest. His lips started to move, as if he wanted to tell me something. I brought my face close to his, and I heard him whisper: "Your Highness, I know I'm going to die. But I'm afraid for you and the Shah." And then he said something I had not expected to hear. He told me that the greatest danger would come not from those who attacked him, but from the followers of Mossadegh. "You must be careful of him," he whispered. His head slumped into the pillow and he died. Hajir's death shook me, for although the political climate of Iran was rarely tranquil, this was the first time I had personally known anyone who had lost his life from such terrorism. The killer was not found, but I believe he was a member of the Islamic Fedayeen, a xenophobic sect.

111

Hajir's death brought me back to the morning of February 4, 1949, when political terror had also struck, but much closer to home. It was a bitter cold winter day that saw the whole city covered with snow, and my brother was scheduled to attend an anniversary ceremony at Teheran University. Since the ranking members of the Tudeh Party, Iran's Moscow-controlled Communist party, had planned a large meeting in the capital the same day, police security was tighter than usual. No one could enter the university grounds without a pass. Government officials, parliamentary representatives, military officials, and members of the press were admitted between the hours of 11 A.M. and 2 P.M. No one noticed the arrival of a young man carrying a cheap camera and a press card issued by a newspaper called *The Flag of Islam*.

At three in the afternoon my brother arrived, in full military dress, and he was greeted by the Chancellor of the University, Dr. Ali Akbar Siasi, as well as the Minister of Education and a delegation of professors. As the military guard stood at ease, the Shah started toward the stairs leading to the main entrance of the university. The photographers all began snapping pictures at a brisk pace—all except Nasser Fakhrarai, the young man from "The Flag of Islam," who stood waiting at the bottom of the stairs.

As my brother came abreast of him, Fakhrarai opened his camera, took out a small revolver, and started shooting. From a distance of only six feet, the assassin fired three shots. By some miracle, the three bullets passed through the Shah's military hat, with only one grazing his scalp. Strangely enough, all the guards scattered, and my brother was left to face his would-be killer alone. A fourth shot hit his cheek and exited through his upper lip. Although he was bleeding profusely, the Shah had the presence of mind to identify the gun as a Belgian Herstell, and he knew it held only six bullets. As my brother started to move around, bobbing and weaving, Fakhrarai aimed the pistol at his heart and fired.

112

This bullet wounded my brother in the shoulder. When the trigger was pulled for the sixth and last shot, the gun jammed. Mohammed Reza Shah was still alive.

Now the crowd sprang into action. Although the Shah shouted at his men to take Fakhrarai alive, the guards killed him on the spot. When it was all over, my brother wanted to continue with the ceremony, but officials convinced him to go to the hospital. I was told that he had been injured, though not seriously, but when I rushed into the hospital and saw him covered with blood, I felt the blood drain from my head and I fainted. I felt embarrassed later when I was told the doctors had left my brother and rushed to revive me, but my reactions to his pain or injury are always visceral and immediate. This is one area in which my attempts at self-control are rarely successful.

My brother's self-control, however, was as unwavering then as it is on almost all occasions. He told me later that after this failed assassination attempt, he had no fear of death; that is a state of mind which I now also share. Since that day in February, my brother has believed that it is God who ordains the moment of death for each human being and that no earthly intervention can either hasten or delay that moment. This belief was strengthened years later, when one day, the Shah was entering the Marble Palace, and one of his own guards opened fire with a machine gun—an attack that left several other guards dead, though the Shah survived, unharmed.

After the first assassination attempt, the police investigation uncovered evidence that Fakhrarai had been a member of the Communist Tudeh Party, a religious fanatic with Marxist views (those who now seem baffled by the emergence of a force called "Islamic Marxism" might take note of the fact that this particular religious-political hybrid has been evolving in our part of the world over the past generation or so, and that it seems to gain in strength whenever there is a period of disenchantment with the West). Thereafter the

Tudeh Party was declared to be illegal, but its members merely took their activities underground and continued to be a strong factor in Iranian politics.

Following the assassination of Prime Minister Hajir, my brother, in June of 1950, appointed General Haj Ali Razmara to Iran's highest political office. Razmara was a professional soldier, a graduate of Saint Cyr who had served for five years as chief of staff. He was not a politician, but he was a capable and energetic administrator, a man who rose at five in the morning and worked tirelessly, often till midnight, a man who was, I knew from my friendship with him, incorruptible and loyal. On the domestic front he made a major contribution in his efforts to clean up and streamline the inefficient and often corrupt bureaucracy.

Equally important, he tried to normalize Iran's relations with all the major powers. Although we were actively building closer ties to the United States, we could never afford to disregard our northern neighbor. As a conciliatory gesture, Razmara allowed the Russians news agency, Tass, to operate freely in Iran, while limiting the activities of the Voice of America and the BBC.

This decision prompted a flurry of accusations and rumors to the effect that Razmara was being subverted by the Russians. I paid no attention to these rumors, nor did I listen to those who suggested that the Prime Minister was a strong, ambitious man who could be dangerous to the monarchy. In matters like this I have always made my judgments intuitively rather than on the basis of any reasoning process. (Even at the end, before the revolution, my intuition about those who would remain loyal to the Shah was almost always correct.) I was certain that Razmara was loyal.

Despite Razmara's attempts to take a conciliatory stance toward the Russians, the Americans trusted him as well because he seemed shrewd enough to hold the country together and to protect it against any serious Communist threat. Yet when he asked the United States for $100 million in economic aid for the rehabilitation of Iran's war-damaged economy, he was offered instead a $25 million loan.

This refusal, and the subsequent departure of various American economic development advisers at a time when Iran badly needed assistance, led to a feeling among Iranians that America had lost interest in helping us. Such a sentiment was easily converted by Mossadegh's National Front followers into a wave of anti-Americanism.

The failure to secure American funds also led Razmara to intensity his efforts to increase Iran's oil income, through a new agreement with Anglo-Iranian oil. ARAMCO had signed a 50–50 agreement with Saudi Arabia during this period, but Anglo-Iranian resisted making a similar arrangement with Iran. This resistance played into the hands of Mossadegh and his followers, who were agitating not for better royalties, but for a complete exclusion of foreign participation and the nationalization of our country's oil. He gathered considerable support for his position, since many Iranians were ready to believe that the oil company was another manifestation of foreign imperialism and was responsible for any number of domestic problems.

Razmara resisted those who pressured him to nationalize Iran's oil. He felt that Iran's financial problems and her lack of technical expertise would make such a move premature and economically disastrous. He continued to push, however, for a 50–50 split of net profits—under the pressure of personal attacks from all sides. On the one hand he was being called a puppet of the oil company because he refused to nationalize; on the other he was being attacked as a Russian agent because of his balanced approach to foreign politics. Joining in these attacks was Ayatollah Kashani; having been elected to parliament in 1950 and chosen as Speaker of the House, Kashani made speeches insisting that Iran's existing oil arrangement—with a foreign power—was against the teachings of the Koran. Thus anyone who opposed the nationalization of oil was an enemy of Islam. Similarly, this reinforced the idea that anyone who was an enemy of Mossadegh was an enemy of Islam.

Razmara came under even heavier fire when a group of Tudeh Party leaders escaped from prison. He was accused by the forces of the right—and in the newspapers that supported them—of having engineered this escape. On March 7, 1951, Haj Ali Razmara attended a ceremony in a Teheran mosque. As he stepped into the courtyard, a bearded young man detached himself from the crowd, stepped behind the Prime Minister, and fired four shots, killing not only Razmara but a nearby policeman. The assassin, Khalil Tahmasebi, tried to commit suicide on the spot, but he was seized and arrested. Ironically, at the time of his murder Razmara had completed a draft of a 50–50 oil agreement.

Khalil Tahmasebi was a carpenter, a Koranic student, and a member of the Islamic Fedayeen, a fanatic organization which denounced all foreigners—from Truman to Stalin to the British royal family—accusing them all of "crimes" against Iran. (If this theme sounds all too familiar today, the reader should bear in mind that a great many movements in Iran are cyclical in nature.) Given the mood of the time, Tahmasebi was never brought to trial and was treated like a national hero by Kashani and his supporters. The newspapers published photographs showing Ayatollah Kashani touching the assassin's beard in a gesture of friendship and approval. It was teachings like those of such Shi'ite leaders as Kashani—teachings that promise a passport to heaven for acts of political terror—which explain the recurrence of such acts throughout contemporary Iranian history.

A few days after Razmara's murder, the Shah appointed as the new Prime Minister Hossein Ala, a capable statesman and diplomat who had served as Iran's Ambassador to the United States and who had presented to the UN Iran's complaint against Russian activity in Azerbaijan. As Prime Minister, Ala proposed that Iran make a compromise agreement whereby the oil industry would be operated by foreign technicians. Mossadegh and his supporters would have none of this. With wild promises of oil revenues of $1 million a day, with the continuing demonstrations which he could summon up at will (with the assistance of his ally, Ayatollah Kashani), Mossadegh forced the resignation of Hossein Ala and created a political climate in which no one but he could be the next Prime Minister. Thus on April 29, 1951, the Shah appointed Dr. Mohammed Mossadegh Prime Minister (but not until Mossadegh had won assurances from the Shah of British support). His first order of business was to settle old scores with the Pahlavis—in particular with me, who he knew had been virulent in my opposition to him in the years of his ascent to power.

On a more personal note, Mossadegh and I had first crossed paths a few years earlier, shortly after I had organized the Imperial Organization for Social Services. I invited him to a meeting at my house to discuss the selection of a board of directors and several other organizational matters.

A servant came into my drawing room to announce the arrival of Dr. Mossadegh. He entered, bowed, and seated himself next to me. I started to talk to him about our board of directors, but his attitude told me that social work was the last thing he wanted to discuss. As soon as he could politely manage it, he turned the subject to oil.

I explained that my brother, like many Iranians, was for the nationalization of oil, provided it was carried out in a rational manner, through proper channels. His answer: "It could be—if you would let it."

Our discussion turned into a direct confrontation when Mossadegh started criticizing my father and brother. He insisted that the Pahlavis had compromised Iran's independence by attempting to modernize the country. When I tried to point out that his views were totally unsupported in reality, he lost control and said: "Your father made a terrible mistake when he built the Trans-Iranian Railroad. If he hadn't done that, Iran wouldn't have been occupied during the war."

This was too much for me to swallow. Fighting to keep my own composure, I rang for a servant and said; "Please show this gentleman out." In the space of one visit Mohammed Mossadegh and I had become enemies. (It may be difficult for Westerners to understand fully how personal grudges of Middle Easterners, some decades old, can outweigh purely political considerations.)

Exactly one hour after his appointment as Prime Minister, Mossadegh sent a message instructing me to leave Iran within 24 hours. My first reaction was to ignore the ultimatum, to challenge Mossadegh's power. But my brother advised me to leave the country.

Unwillingly, I took my children (in addition to Shahram, I now had two children with Shafiq) and left Iran—the start of my second exile, but this one not self-imposed and one that was to keep me from my country and my brother for years.

# MOHAMMED MOSSADEGH

The years of Mossadegh's control over Iran were extremely difficult ones for my brother. My exile left him isolated at exactly the time when the new Prime Minister had cut him off from the government. And before long Mossadegh would attempt his ultimate plan—removing the Shah from his throne. The only comfort he had during that time was the companionship and loyalty of a new wife, whom he had married a few months before I left for Paris and before his power faced the most serious threat since he became Shah.

His bride was Soraya Esfandiari, a member of the influential Bakhtiari tribe who inhabited the central and southern regions of Iran. Her father, Khalil, had helped my father bring the tribal chieftains under the control of the Teheran government.

In 1924 Khalil Esfandiari went to Berlin as a student, and a year later he married a German woman who had been born in Moscow. Khalil and his wife Eva had a daughter in 1932. When Soraya was a child of eight, her parents came back to Iran.

After her life in Europe, however, Eva no longer wished to stay in Iran, and when Soraya was 15, her parents moved to Switzerland. She was sent to a boarding school in Montreux and later to Les Rosseaux school in Lausanne. By the time she was 18, Soraya was a tall, dark beauty with almond-shaped green eyes, an accomplished young woman who could speak German, French, and Persian. Later she would add English to her repertory of languages.

Shams took the first step in arranging this royal match when she met with Soraya in her London hotel and told her, discreetly of course, that it would be wonderful for our brother to have a wife like her. Soraya seemed quite receptive to the idea, and she agreed to come to Teheran with her father. A "casual" meeting was arranged at my mother's home. That first meeting went very well; my brother seemed quite taken with her and she seemed to enjoy the first few hours they spent together. Everything moved very quickly; an engagement was announced almost immediately, and a wedding was scheduled for December 27, 1950.

In the days preceding the wedding, the Shah and Soraya found that they shared an enthusiasm for outdoor sports, especially horseback riding. Late one afternoon, after a long and vigorous riding session, Soraya developed a very high fever. The following morning, what first seemed to be a normal cold was diagnosed as typhoid fever. My brother rushed Soraya to the hospital and called in several of the best doctors in Teheran.

Although almost a quarter century had elapsed since the Shah's childhood bout with the disease, typhoid was still a potential killer. Each day, my brother would leave his office for an hour or so, just as my father had done so many years before, to sit in the hospital at his fiancée's bedside. He watched her condition deteriorate. She was delirious most of the time, and her life seemed to be in serious danger until the Shah's personal physician remembered that he had read about a new drug called "aureomycin." A supply of the drug

120

was flown to Teheran from the United States, and Soraya's life was miraculously saved.

Complete recovery was very slow. She was weak and pale for weeks, not in any condition to go through a long, formal marriage ceremony. The date was postponed to February 12, but unexpectedly Soraya suffered a relapse. Since typhoid is an intestinal disease, the patient must remain on a strict diet until recovery is complete. One of Soraya's friends had sent her a box of chocolates from Switzerland, and without stopping to think, she ate most of the candy. Her symptoms returned, leaving her thoroughly debilitated. However, the decision was made—no doubt because of political uncertainties—not to postpone the wedding again.

We tried to scale down the ceremonies and festivities to more manageable proportions so Soraya's strength would not be taxed any more than was absolutely necessary. The site of the wedding was changed from the Golestan Palace to the Marble Palace, which was smaller, less formal, and much easier to heat. Teheran winter days can be bitingly cold. The Muslim ceremony was cut to a minimum, and the festivities would be held on the same day. Originally we had planned a gala celebration with a large international guest list; but it was reduced to two very old, very dear family friends, the Agha Khan and his wife Beygum, members of the court, the Shah's ministers, the diplomatic corps, several clergymen, and of course family members.

February 12 was a very cold day, the city blanketed under a heavy layer of snow. Soraya's gown, a Dior silver-lamé and brocade creation with a magnificent train, weighed almost 50 pounds, and the poor girl almost collapsed before she reached the Marble Palace. The ceremony was a simple one, performed according to ancient Persian tradition. The bride and groom were seated on a sofa facing a tablecloth decorated with symbolic objects: a mirror, two silver and gold candlesticks, a large Iranian bread, eggs, herbs, a

Koran, Persian sweets, *nabat* (a Persian candy made with crystallized sugar), and gold coins. These represent health, happiness, faith, prosperity, and sweetness.

The mullah began by asking Soraya if she was willing to become the Shah's lawful wife. Traditionally the bride doesn't answer this question until it has been asked three times (so as not to seem overeager or immodest), and then only in a low, demure voice. Once the answer is given, the wedding guests shower the bridal couple with gold coins and candies, which are then picked up by the young single girls, because these items are said to bring good luck.

After this religious ceremony, we all moved into the next room for a formal presentation of the wedding gifts, which included a crystal bowl from Harry Truman, a sable coat from Stalin, and a set of crystal vases from me.

I was happy to see my brother marry a woman he obviously loved very deeply, but we were all feeling more apprehensive than festive that day. Several times Soraya seemed on the verge of fainting, and when the royal wedding banquet (which naturally included our native Iranian caviar) was over, we were all relieved that the bride was still on her feet. The following morning the newlyweds left for a resort area on the Caspian coast, where they would stay until Soraya was completely well; then they would fly to Europe for an extended honeymoon.

I was sent into exile a few weeks after Soraya and my brother returned, so I didn't have an opportunity to get to know my new sister-in-law. But in the short time we were in Teheran together, I did get the feeling that she preferred to keep her relationship with her in-laws on a fairly formal basis. Since my brother was very much in love with her, I tried to keep my distance unless I was invited to visit. Again this became the focus of the local gossip circuit in Teheran, and rumors flew that this desire for privacy and independence on Soraya's part was meant to show her open hostility toward me. Later, even though I was living in Europe during the years that Soraya was trying unsuccessfully to have a child, the gossip mongers went so far—I knew then they would stop at nothing—as to suggest that I had given her drugs to make her sterile.

My three-year exile in Paris was at one and the same time the most painful and the happiest period of my life. When I first arrived in France, I felt as if my life had completely fallen apart. I was separated from my brother, deprived of the work that had given me so much purpose and meaning, and forced to live in a country where I had no family and few friends. Shafiq had not offered to share my exile, and I had not asked him.

After six years of marriage we had a relationship that was correct, but cool. We had started our life together amicably enough, each of us with work that was absorbing and challenging, both of us enjoying the leisure time we shared together. We had (in addition to my son from my first marriage) a son, Shahriar, and a daughter, Azadeh.

Ours should have been a happy family, and if it was less than that, then I feel the fault was mine. No matter what else a woman does, whether she is a princess, a politician, a scientist, or a teacher, I believe she plays the critical role in creating (or not creating) the solidarity of a family. Ideally I feel that being a wife is a full-time job; but I, like many young women today, was not willing to make it one.

Like many men, especially Oriental men, my husband needed to be given attention and respect, to be treated as head of the household. My active political and social life kept me from being fully responsive to these needs. I simply could not be what is called by some in America the "total wife." The only thing that keeps me from feeling guilty about this failure is the certainty that my husband knew basically what kind of woman he was marrying. We had the kind of marriage that evolves when one partner has a career, like politics or the arts, that becomes more and more demanding.

Such a marriage can never be easy, but I think it is especially hard when the partner who is more active or more often in the public eye is the wife.

My husband felt neglected and unappreciated, and with his very good looks he had no problem finding consolation with other women. I think I must have sensed that Shafiq was unfaithful, but I never voiced these suspicions. I hate marital confrontations or family fights of any kind. I believe very strongly that husband and wife should either find a way to live peacefully, or they should separate peacefully. And I suppose there was that element of doubt; as long as I didn't know for a certainty that Shafiq had other women, I could always say to myself: "No, it isn't really true—he wouldn't dare—not here in Teheran."

The doubt ended when the husband of one of Shafiq's mistresses came to me and said our spouses had been lovers for some time. I can't say that my heart was broken, since Shafiq and I had never been madly in love. But I was hurt and more than a little humiliated to have a stranger bring me news of his infidelities.

When I confronted Shafiq with the man's accusation, he admitted the truth of it, very calmly and in such a way as to let me know that his affairs would probably continue.

With two small children from this marriage, plus one failed marriage already, I didn't really think about divorce, at least not at that point. Rather our marriage became an "arrangement"—polite, correct, and distant. When I left Teheran for Paris with Shahriar, who was six, and Azadeh, who was six months, Shafiq and I had no discussion about when we might see each other again. (As it happened, he made three visits during the three-year period.) Our farewell was like one between two distant cousins, many times removed.

My first home in Paris was the Diana Hotel on George V Avenue, a small hotel in a quiet neighborhood. Here at last I was living in the Paris of my girlhood dreams, except these were not exactly the circumstances I had dreamed of. I realized almost at once that living in Paris, even a fairly simple life, was going to be much more expensive than living in Teheran, and that the money I had brought with me was not going to last very long.

In later years, after the value of lands in Iran multiplied a thousandfold, the land holdings I had inherited from my father would make me a rich woman. But when I left Teheran, what money I did have was frozen in Iranian banks—the government had recently enacted a series of strict regulations governing the transfer of exchange—and since the Iranian *rial* had suffered severe devaluation against the dollar and the French franc, the amount I had brought with me shrank alarmingly when converted into local currency.

I didn't want to ask my husband for financial assistance, and any transfer of my brother's funds to me would no doubt have caused political fireworks. So I wrote instead to my mother and sister Shams, asking them to sell my house and send me the proceeds. Unfortunately the real estate market then was so sluggish that no buyers were found. It was bought later, during the tenure of Prime Minister Zahedi, when it became the office of the Premier and the official meeting place for the Council of Ministers.

My financial situation went from difficult to rather desperate when my son Shahriar was stricken with a bone disease. I was terrified that he had either cancer or bone tuberculosis and was relieved when I found out he didn't. But he did have a rare bone disease that would have to be treated in a specialized hospital in Zurich. Although it may be hard to believe, at that time I simply did not have the money to pay for this treatment, and I didn't know how I would get it.

This was the only time in my life that I had severe financial problems, and I didn't have the slightest idea how I would solve them in a foreign country, cut off from whatever resources I had. I became depressed and confused and restless. I had always had difficulty sleeping, even as a child, but now I would spend entire nights wide awake and miserable.

It was then that I started spending my nights in casinos, not as a way of enjoying myself but for the same reasons that people sometimes drink too much or take drugs—to avoid facing reality, even when they can ill afford it. I quickly lost the money I had left, and the shock of what I had done was enough to keep me away from the gaming tables for a very long time.

The "Iranian grapevine," which operates as effectively abroad as it does at home, came to my rescue. An old friend, an Iranian rug merchant named Jahangir Jahangiri, heard of my son's illness and my financial condition. He phoned me from Zurich, where he was living at the time, and offered to pay transportation and hospital bills and to lend me some money for living expenses. I accepted his offer with relief and gratitude and left for Switzerland immediately with Shahriar.

Shortly after I settled him in the hospital in Zurich, I returned to Paris and moved into an apartment on avenue de Montespan. The house was an old one with windows overlooking an inner courtyard. A hundred years before, the courtyard had served as a "parking lot" for coaches, and one of these old coaches still sat there, a decaying souvenir of old France. Now that my worries had eased, I felt relaxed enough to enjoy the simple pleasure of looking out the window and daydreaming about what Paris might have been like in the nineteenth century, or even at the time Madame Arfa was telling me her wonderful stories.

It was during this period that I met Mehdi Bushehri, the man who would become my third and present husband. I had gone, with a young Iranian woman I had met in Paris, to a small café for afternoon tea. Two young men were sitting at the table next to ours; one of them, a Frenchman, seemed to know my companion, and he came over to greet us. After an exchange of small talk, he asked if he might introduce his friend, Mehdi Bushehri. I was quite surprised when I heard the Iranian name because the man at the table was fair-skinned with blond hair and brown eyes and altogether very European looking.

When Mehdi came to our table, he told us, in very good French, that he was studying at Paris University and that his favorite subjects were literature, art, cinema, and theater. I liked him at once, and the hour or two of our first meeting went by quickly. When my friend and I got up to leave, Mehdi asked if he could see me again. I agreed at once, without a hint of the reserve or hesitation that women of my generation were taught.

Mehdi's mother was from the Caucasus and his father was a well-known businessman in southern Iran. The family name, in fact, was derived from the name of a southern port and dated back only to my father's reign; before then, many Iranians had only first names, being known as "Farid, son of Ali," or some similar designation. When my father said that everyone had to choose a family name, Mehdi's father borrowed his from the port of Bushehr, where he did much of his shipping.

Mehdi completely changed my life in Paris. One day I had felt all alone in a foreign country; then suddenly I had a new friend, one who opened up the whole city for me. We went to museums, theaters, and little out-of-the-way movie houses, where Mehdi always knew what was playing.

After we discovered that we shared a special interest in jazz, Mehdi took me often to a club called Vieux Columbier. We would sit there for hours and listen to Sidney Bechet, the white-haired black clarinetist, play New Orleans Dixieland.

Without knowing it, Mehdi gave me a precious gift, the wish that had been denied me two decades earlier, to live like a student in Paris. Years before, my father had said "no" to a European university, and now I quite unexpectedly had a

127

second chance, one I could share with a man whose company was a constant source of pleasure. Mehdi brought me books, the works of European authors like Moravia, Camus, Gide, Sartre (who was very popular then among European intellectuals), and Malraux. After I read the books, Mehdi and I would discuss and compare them, especially the works of Sartre and Malraux.

Many years later I would meet Malraux at an Iranian Embassy reception in Paris, just two weeks after he had lost his two young sons in a tragic car accident. I longed to speak to him, but I didn't know what to say. As I stood watching Malraux, and wondering how he could be so calm and self-possessed in the face of such tragedy, he walked over to me and started talking about Iranian culture and art, about the city of Isfahan, which he said was one of the seven most interesting cities in the world. When he saw how amazed I was that he could talk so calmly and abstractly at a time when his personal life must have been extremely painful, he said to me: "I want you to know that I am weeping inside for my children, but I simply don't belong only to myself any more. I have accepted certain responsibilities which make me carry on regardless of my personal problems and feelings." I didn't really understand what Malraux was saying; the scope of my own personal tragedies had been fairly limited. Understanding would come later, only after I too had lost my country and my son.

Now, I look back at those later Paris years as the happiest and freest of my life. Mehdi and I saw each other almost every day, and I found that he had become an important and necessary part of my life. For the first time since I had lost Houshang, I was in love again. But this time there was a difference: Mehdi had become a dear and trusted friend, a man who even today I cannot fault in any way.

Together we experienced Paris during one of its most exciting and vital periods. It was still the Paris that had attracted intellectuals and bohemians and artists and lovers for so many generations, but now it was starting to show traces of what the French called "Coca-colonization." Nylon stockings were replacing silk, and French housewives were talking about supermarkets, vacuum cleaners, washing machines, and television sets.

The cultural life of the city reflected this mix of old and new. One of the dance companies Mehdi and I loved to watch was Les Ballet du Marquis de Cuevas, a troupe that displayed as much panache offstage as it did while performing. The manager of this company liked to tour in the grand old manner, taking his Louis XVI bed, twenty dogs, and six personal physicians on every engagement. Quite understandably, the troupe eventually went bankrupt.

The "new wave" of French art was most evident in the work of new film makers, especially directors like Roger Vadim. This man had made several exciting films, and when an Iranian friend, Dominique Seif, invited me to a party at Vadim's home, I accepted with pleasure and some curiosity. When I arrived at Vadim's home, a large apartment located on St. Germain des Prés, I recognized a number of film actors, including Marlon Brando, who was there with a friend of mine. I was wearing the sable coat Stalin had given me years before, and later when Brando and our mutual friend dropped me off at home in a taxi, he startled me by saying: "You are very attractive, but the coat you're wearing makes me think you are either a very rich woman or a rich man's mistress."

I froze for a moment.

"You don't seem to know who I am," he said.

"On the contrary, Mr. Brando, I know you very well. But apparently you don't know who *I* am."

I can't say that I was very surprised when Mehdi asked me to marry him, but I felt that we couldn't make any plans until I was free to go back to Iran and resolve the question of my marriage with Shafiq.

From what I was hearing and reading, however, it seemed as if there was very little good news from Iran. My brother was daily losing ground to Mossadegh, whose dramatic gestures delighted the mobs he liked to rally, but were crippling the Iranian economy.

The day after he was sworn in as Prime Minister, he pushed the nationalization of oil bill through the Parliament (April 30, 1951) amidst a mood of national excitement that bordered on delirium. It was as if the people imagined that suddenly all the wealth that was going to the foreign oil company would revert to Iran. Certainly the sums in question were enormous. In 1950, for example, the Iranian share of oil revenues was 16 million pounds (which represented half the national budget), while Anglo-Iranian's share was five times that amount.

Yet what happened after the nationalization move was not a wave of instant prosperity, but a show of solidarity by the major oil companies (the "Seven Sisters") that brought Iran to its knees.

Mossadegh's scheme backfired. When he nationalized the oil industry, he expelled all British technicians—in the expectation that he could keep the oil fields operating with help that would come from America. Mossadegh had good reason for these expectations: the United States had actively supported his appointment as Prime Minister, and the American Ambassador in Teheran, Henry Grady, had encouraged him on the issue of oil nationalization (no doubt with the hope of gaining an advantage over the British).

But American support failed to materialize, and together with the Anglo-Iranian Oil Company (and the other "Sisters"), America's oil companies boycotted Iranian oil, filling the gap in supplies by stepping up production in Kuwait, Saudi Arabia, Bahrain, and Iraq. Even when the price of Iranian oil was slashed, from $1.70 a barrel to $.90, in a desperate effort to find customers, only one small Italian company called Supor took advantage of the offer. One oil tanker—Rosemary—was sent to Abadan and left the port after a rather pathetic ceremony. The tanker was confiscated in the port of Aden by the Royal British Air Force, which claimed that the cargo belonged to Anglo-Iranian. After that incident, there were no more foreign customers for Iranian oil.

Mossadegh remained popular, though, thanks to several dramatic gestures which distracted the people from the severe economic problems that were ahead. While his erstwhile ally, Ayatollah Kashani, was stirring up crowds by preaching a doctrine of Pan-Islamism (which would be supported, he said, by a worldwide Muslim army), Mossadegh made public a list of politicians who had allegedly taken gifts from the oil company. Here we see an example—like the one we would see almost 30 years later—of how an economic crisis can be obscured by the mobilizing of anti-foreign sentiment.

The Anglo-Iranian Oil Company had appealed to the International Court of Justice at the Hague, and the court had made a provisional ruling asking the interested parties to respect the status quo until a final settlement could be reached. In an attempt to mediate such a settlement, President Truman sent his special envoy, Averell Harriman, to Teheran—a move that provoked anti-American demonstrations by the very active underground left.

The British then submitted a resolution to the UN Security Council which, if passed, would force Iran to accept the ruling of the Hague Court. It was then that Mossadegh made his trip to New York, in October 1951, when he addressed the UN Security Council. During his stay in America, Mossadegh met and apparently charmed Dean Acheson, the U.S. Secretary of State, an aristocratic-looking gentleman who looked like a British diplomat but who had a strong antipathy for British imperialism. Mossadegh managed to put on a show that UN members would long remember (some said he made a fool of himself and embarrassed Iran, but he was a speaker who could mesmerize an audience). To make his point and to impress his listeners with his sincerity, Mossadegh would weep regularly, drying his tears with the "Old Mossie" handkerchiefs that became his trademark, and would whip himself into a frenzy of emotion until he fainted, or seemed on the verge of collapse.

Although he made a vivid presentation of Iran's case for nationalization, Mossadegh left the United States no nearer to an oil settlement than when he arrived. At home the economic situation was deteriorating by the day: the government had been unable to meet its payroll for weeks, the army was being given token pay, and inflation was exacerbated by paper money the Prime Minister was printing in order to put more rials into circulation.

In an effort to stave off the erosion of his support, Mossadegh went to the Parliament in July 1952 and said he could solve Iran's problems if he was given six months of absolute power. Parliament refused, and Mossadegh resigned. My brother then appointed Ahmad Qavam to replace him. Although Qavam had often opposed my brother during his previous tenure as Prime Minister, the Shah chose him because he felt that Qavam might be the one man strong enough to create a viable government. But he was wrong. Qavam was now old and ill and simply not equal to the enormous pressures of the day. Hundreds of thousands of demonstrators screamed for Mossadegh and demanded Qavam's resignation. In the ensuing disorder, many homes and buildings, including Qavam's residence, were burned. The Shah had no choice but to accept Qavam's resignation, reappoint Mossadegh, and comply with all his demands.

Now Mossadegh became bolder and made my brother a virtual prisoner in his own palace. He even tapped his phone and infiltrated the royal court with informers. Mossadegh then delivered a final insult, demanding that he be given the function of Commander-in-Chief of the army, a prerogative that has always belonged to the throne. When my brother refused, Mossadegh decided to try another bold move: he "suggested" to the Shah that he leave the country on an extended vacation (as the Qajar kings used to do). Later, my brother told me that he had in fact decided to leave the country on February 26, 1953, but he changed his mind when he saw a noisy demonstration outside the palace, with people chanting pro-Shah slogans and demanding that he stay.

Ironically, we found out later that this demonstration had been organized by some of the religious leaders who had originally supported Mossadegh but who were now having second thoughts about his considerable power and about his flirtation with the Tudeh Party and the forces of the left. Since he had come into power, Mossadegh had increasingly disregarded his clerical supporters and turned more and more to the well-organized, well-financed Communist groups in Iran. Although these had been outlawed in 1946, the Russians always felt they could one day bring Iran into the Soviet bloc, *if* they could first topple the Shah.

Not only the mullahs, but the Americans also were having second thoughts about Mossadegh. Under the Truman Administration, Secretary of State Dean Acheson had supported Mossadegh because the Americans saw him as a strong and powerful politician who could hold the line against Communist infiltration. Now America had a new President, Dwight D. Eisenhower, and a new Secretary of State, John Foster Dulles. Dulles, unlike Acheson, saw politics almost as a religion, judging political issues as "right" or "wrong," with very little room for compromise. He worked as if he had an important mission to accomplish within a very short time, with little margin for error.

In the spring of 1953, America was winding down the war in Korea and the official attitude was, as one State Department source put it, of "waiting for the dust to settle in Korea and the sky to clear in Iran."

When the dust did settle and the sky did clear, there

was good reason for alarm: Iran seemed to be headed straight for the Soviet bloc. On May 1 a massive leftist demonstration was held in front of the Iranian Parliament. From the loudspeakers installed throughout the plaza came voices which incited the crowds with slogans like: "Long live the great people of Korea and China. We greet the heroic people of the U.S.S.R., who are at the helm of the democratic world. Death to the United States! Death to Great Britain!"

This set the tone for similar demonstrations in the near future which would have less and less to do with oil or domestic problems and would focus instead on whipping up anti-American and anti-British sentiments. It was time, the Americans decided, to intervene.

During the summer of 1953 an Iranian whose name I can't reveal—I will call him Mr. B.—phoned and said he had an urgent message for me. When we met, he said that the United States and Great Britain were extremely concerned about the current situation in Iran and that they had devised a plan to solve the problem and benefit the Shah. He added that my assistance was needed before this plan could be put into operation. When I asked for details, he said that these would be explained if I agreed to meet two men—an American and an Englishman—whose names he could not tell me.

Since I knew Mr. B. very well, I was aware that he carried two passports, one Iranian and one American, and that he had contacts with high-level American officials. Because I trusted him, I agreed to listen.

Within 24 hours the phone rang again. This time it was an American who introduced himself only as a friend of Mr. B. and asked me to come to the Cascade Restaurant in Boulogne at four o'clock the following afternoon. When I asked him how I would recognize him, he said he knew what I looked like and he would make contact with me.

The next day I arrived at the restaurant by taxi, and as soon as I walked in the door, two men rushed forward and greeted me as if we were old friends. We all sat down and ordered tea.

Knowing that my brother's situation was extremely serious, I was very anxious to hear what would be said. "What do you gentlemen have in mind?" I asked, without any preliminary discussion.

The American shook his head. "Not here, Your Highness. We'll have to go somewhere else to talk."

So we sipped our tea and made small talk, apparently for the benefit of anyone who might be watching. Then we drove together to an apartment in a residential building near Saint Cloud. It was only when we were inside that the American told me he was the personal representative of John Foster Dulles and that the Englishman was speaking for Winston Churchill, whose Conservative Party had recently come into power.

When I heard this, I couldn't resist saying: "I want you to give my best regards to John Foster Dulles. Tell him that Mossadegh is the genie that America released from the bottle. Now that he has created problems for you, I can see that you are trying to force him back into the bottle." I have, unfortunately, a tendency always to say what I'm thinking, even in delicate political or diplomatic situations. This lack of restraint often gets me into trouble, but in this instance no one seemed to be offended.

"I agree with you," said the American, "and that is exactly why we are here—to do something about this mutual problem." He assured me that he was speaking in good faith and added: "Our intelligence shows us that the Shah is still popular with the people. Although the head of the army, General Riahi, supports Mossadegh, the majority of officers and troops are loyal to the Shah."

The Englishman, who had been relatively silent until then, said: "This is the time for action, but we must ask for your help. If you accept the mission, we can give you the details." He paused for a moment and then continued.

135

"Since we are asking you to risk your life, we will provide you with a blank check. You can fill in whatever amount you wish."

I was so stunned I didn't even hear the rest of what he was saying. Although I had very limited funds at this time, the suggestion that I would take money for an operation that would help my country made me lose my temper. "None of us seems to understand each other," I said, "so there is no point in continuing this discussion. Now—will you give me a ride back or shall I call a taxi?"

The next day I received a huge basket of flowers, with no card. It was followed by a visit from Mr. B., who said he wanted to apologize for the misunderstanding. He asked me to come to another meeting.

This time our meeting place was a road in the Bois de Boulogne. I was told to look for a particular make and color of car which would be waiting for me. Once again, I was driven to the apartment near Saint Cloud. The two gentlemen reopened our discussion, with some caution so as not to hurt my feelings again. They explained that the first step in their plan was to find an absolutely reliable way of getting a message to the Shah. Since they had to be sure that the courier could be trusted, that there would be no possibility of a leak, they thought of me. At the time Great Britain had no ambassador in Iran and the mission had to be carried out outside of regular American diplomatic channels.

"Are you gentlemen aware that I've been sent into exile? I have no valid passport that I can use to enter Iran."

"Just leave that detail to us," said the American. "Will you do this—for your brother?"

"Of course. How soon can you put me on an airplane?"

"The day after tomorrow."

The American gave me an Air France flight number and instructed me to be at Orly Airport just before flight time so I could be given a ticket.

Was there anyone in Iran that I could trust? the American asked. I gave them the name of a woman friend. Later I sent this woman a coded cable, telling her I might be in Teheran soon. The only other person who knew about my departure was Mehdi; I phoned him and simply said I had to be out of Paris for a while.

Two days later, on a rainy day in early July, I arrived at the Orly departure terminal wearing a gray two-piece suit and carrying a single small suitcase. I sensed almost immediately that I wasn't alone. A porter approached me, took my bag, and told me to follow him. As I glanced briefly around, I felt the protective presence of a circle of people near me. Within a few moments, several of the other passengers saw it too, and they started pointing and whispering, apparently trying to guess what was going on.

The porter led me through a door and down a long corridor to a waiting car, which took me directly to the airplane. I was handed a boarding pass and an envelope, which I was to give only to my brother. As soon as I took my seat on the plane, I noticed two men who were obviously there to protect me—or rather the envelope I was carrying. The plane took off, exactly on time. I was relieved that the flight had not been delayed, since Teheran was then under martial law. If we were to land after dark, there might be no way to get home. All through the eight-hour flight to Teheran, I kept asking myself the same questions. What if one of Mossadegh's people recognized me at the airport? What if I were to be arrested? How would I explain this illicit reentry into Iran—and the absence of a French exit stamp on my passport? If I were intercepted at the airport, the entire operation might be aborted; we could have a major political scandal—and Mossadegh would have yet another weapon in his move to unseat the Shah.

Getting off that plane in Teheran was an experience I'll never forget. I had very little fear for my personal safety, but there was so much at stake that I was trembling from head to toe as I walked down the steps to the runway. The first person I saw was the woman friend I had cabled. She walked toward me, took my arm, and casually directed me away from the other passengers who were walking toward the terminal. A taxi was waiting for us in a dark corner of the runway, but I could see at once that this was not an ordinary taxi. Taxis were not permitted on airport runways and the driver seemed to know my friend quite well.

Once again I left an airport without passing through customs, and once again I held my breath as we moved away from the airport. I don't think a dozen words were exchanged in the tense atmosphere of that car ride since all three of us were now subject to very harsh reprisals if we were to be recognized and stopped.

I was taken directly to the house of one of my half brothers, a villa inside the Saadabad Palace compound. He and his wife welcomed me, but they did not ask for any explanation of this very irregular visit. They said that the Shah was well but that the political situation in Teheran was extremely unstable and the tension between my brother and Mossadegh had reached crisis proportions.

Within half an hour of my arrival, a servant hurried into the drawing room and said that the Teheran Martial Law Governor wanted to see me. The Governor came in, saluted me and said: "Your Highness, the Prime Minister has been informed of your arrival in Teheran. The Air France plane has been ordered to stay at the airport to take you out of the country immediately."

Now that I had actually reached my destination, I was not about to leave before I delivered the crucial envelope to my brother. I took a chance and risked all: "Tell your master to go to hell. I am an Iranian, and I will stay in my own country as long as I wish. I have come back only to get some funds to pay my son's hospital expenses. If you want to arrest me, go right ahead, but you cannot simply order me to leave the country."

The Governor left without answering. An hour later he was back. "I have relayed your message to the Prime Minister," he said. "He has granted you permission to stay in Iran for 24 hours—but no more. All government bureaus have been instructed to assist you in whatever you have to do here. I must also ask you not to leave this house without the guards and escort we have assigned to you. After 24 hours, this escort will take you to the airport." Now I was officially under house arrest.

I did, however, have one small edge in this confrontation with Mossadegh. The Saadabad Palace compound was normally surrounded by the Imperial Guards, commanded at that time by Colonel Nematollah Nassiry, and they are traditionally loyal to the Shah and the Royal Family. After I was placed under house arrest, soldiers of the Iranian army (commanded by General Riahi, Mossadegh's Chief of Staff) formed another circle, surrounding the Imperial Guard. I knew that if these troops tried to enter the palace grounds and take me by force, there would be a military confrontation; I felt reasonably certain that Mossadegh would try to avoid this kind of direct warfare with the Royal Family.

That evening the Minister of Court, Abolghassem Amini (a Mossadegh supporter) visited the Shah and convinced him that in order to appease Mossadegh, he would be well advised to issue an official announcement dissociating himself from my visit, which had already made headlines in Teheran. The announcement, which was published in the the newspapers and read on the radio, said: "The Imperial Court of Iran hereby announces that Princess Ashraf has entered the country without prior permission and approval from the Shah. She has been requested to leave the country immediately after attending to some personal business."

Although the announcement was harsh in tone, I understood that my brother had no choice in this matter. I had come to Iran to help him, not to push him into a premature confrontation with Mossadegh on my behalf. If there was anything I had learned in 34 years of living, it was that I was perfectly capable of taking care of myself.

The following day a servant brought word that Queen Soraya would come later that afternoon to the garden behind the house where I was staying at Saadabad. I watched from the window. As soon as I saw my sister-in-law approach, I walked outside, quickly handed her the envelope and went back inside (I still cannot reveal the contents of that fateful letter.) I remained in Iran for nine more days, ostensibly attending to personal and financial matters.

During those days Saadabad, which was originally the Royal Family's summer palace, became my personal fortress. (A few years later, it would become my home.) The palace compound, located at the foothills of the Alborz Mountains (about 5,200 meters above sea level), some 60 kilometers east of Teheran, covers a broad area divided by a fast-running stream which can be crossed by small bridges. Scattered among the tall, stately trees are several brick houses used by members of the Royal Family. Although I was not able to see my brother—any meeting between us at this time would have been dangerous—I did have the comforting presence of other family members.

Although I wished desperately that I could stay and be near my brother through whatever was ahead, I realized that there was no other course but to go back into exile.

Ten days to the day after my arrival, a military escort took me to Teheran airport, where I boarded an Air France plane for my return to Paris.

Soon after I returned to France, I decided to set up housekeeping on my husband Shafiq's boat, which was anchored at Cannes. Shafiq had bought the yacht—originally called the "Roma"—in London, changed the name to "Khorramshahr," and brought it to Cannes. When the port master saw me approaching with my suitcase, he said; "Your Highness, if you are intending to go aboard, I must tell you that the boat is not in liveable condition."

I saw at once that his statement was depressingly accurate. The boat hadn't been used in two years, and the signs of neglect were everywhere. The living quarters were waterlogged, the paint rusted, the engine inoperable, the supply of bottled gas depleted. The sheets and curtains were moldy, and a thick layer of dust and cobwebs covered all the furnishings.

The harbor master said that for 2,000 francs he could make the boat habitable within 24 hours. I told him to go ahead, checked into a small hotel next door, and phoned a French gentleman friend to come and give me a hand.

The following morning we met at the boat, rolled up our sleeves, and joined the two workmen who were already busy scrubbing and scraping. As we worked, we listened to the shortwave radio my friend had brought me. Suddenly the announcer's voice on the BBC broadcast said there had been a bulletin from Radio Teheran: after a failed *coup d'état* the Shah and Queen Soraya had fled the country in a small plane.

"My God—what's happened?" I said. But there was no more news. Subsequent bulletins said first that the Shah had landed in Baghdad and later that he was at the Excelsior Hotel in Rome. But none of these reports answered all the questions I had. What was this attempted *coup d'état*? Was this the plan that Mr. B.'s friends had seemed so confident about? What had gone wrong? I could hardly contain my frustration, my need to see my brother, and to know more than these radio bulletins were telling me.

On the morning of August 18 I placed a call to the Hotel Excelsior and learned from my brother that there had been no attempted coup, but that he could not tell me any more on the telephone. I told him that I would join him in Rome.

141

As soon as I hung up, I called a French friend. "I must get to Rome as quickly as possible. What would you suggest?"

"Don't you know there is a transportation strike?" he answered. "There are no trains or planes out of here."

"Well, I still mean to get to Rome, and since I can't walk, let's try to think of an alternative."

"My Peugeot is fairly fast. Shall I drive you?"

"I'd be very grateful if you would. When can we leave?"

"Just give me a few hours to have the car checked and filled with petrol."

At two o'clock that afternoon we took the road heading for the Italian border. As we passed Nice, I realized that I had no Italian visa. "Do you think we'll have any problems when we get to the border?" I asked.

He thought for a moment. "I think there's a good chance that we'll get through. The border guards usually check the car and the driver. Since I'm French, we may be all right."

When we reached the border it was raining heavily, and the guard didn't seem anxious to leave his shelter. My friend got out of the car, presented his identity card, and we were waved through the barrier.

The border road is lined with bougainvilleas and geraniums, but that day the clouds and rain made the landscape gray and monotonous. I wanted to drive all night (I am normally a "night person" who stays up until three or four in the morning), but I was afraid my friend would fall asleep at the wheel. I turned on the radio and kept up a steady stream of conversation until we got very tired. We decided to stop to get something to eat and take a one-hour nap in the parking lot of the restaurant.

At five in the morning we were awakened by the sound of a truck engine, and after a quick cup of coffee, we were on the road again. I remember that we had just passed a long stretch of mountain road when the music on the radio stopped and a voice announced: "In the latest news from Teheran there have been massive demonstrations in support of the Shah. Military personnel carrying pro-Shah banners have attacked government offices and the home of Dr. Mossadegh. General Zahedi, the Prime Minister designated by the Shah, has come out of hiding, and his followers have occupied the radio station in Teheran." This news was like a miraculous shot of adrenaline, and I still don't know how I contained myself in that small car.

We reached Rome very late on the evening of the 19th, so I didn't get to the Excelsior until the following morning. I found my brother surrounded by journalists, but when he saw me, he drew me to him and said to the reporters, "This is my sister Ashraf, whom all of you know."

Later, when we were alone, he told me the entire sequence of events starting on August 13, when he had written a *firman*—an imperial decree—dismissing Mossadegh as Prime Minister and replacing him with General Fazlollah Zahedi. He had given the extremely delicate—and dangerous—job of delivering the *firman* to Colonel Nassiry, commander of the Imperial Guard. When Nassiry took the decree to the Prime Minister, Mossadegh had him arrested—and had issued the news that the Shah's attempted coup had failed. It was at that point that my brother flew his small private plane from the Caspian Sea, where he and Soraya had been staying, to Baghdad.

Several anxious days followed, for if Mossadegh was not to succeed in his plot to dethrone the Shah, then the people had to be told exactly what had happened. And here apparently is where the plan—"Operation Ajax"—that "Mr. B." had alluded to in Paris went into operation.

A great deal has been written about "Operation Ajax" since 1953, much of it implying that this was a military operation by which the American CIA forcibly restored the Shah to his throne. "Ajax" was, as far as I know, not a military operation, but an information operation. It cost the

CIA almost $60,000 for the part they played in the counter-coup. (I later learned that they had been willing to spend up to $1 million to topple Mossadegh.) After Nassiry's arrest, the pro-Shah forces in Iran found a printing plant which would, for a price, print tens of thousands of flyers and posters reproducing the text of my brother's decree dismissing Mossadegh. Within two days these were distributed throughout Teheran, demonstrating to the people that it was Mossadegh who had committed an act of treason against the Crown, and rallying a great surge of popular support for the Shah.

After I spent some time with my brother, I made preparations to go back to Cannes for a few days before I ended my two years of exile. I received a call from our Ambassador to Rome, who asked me to see him. Normally this was the kind of courtesy call I would have accepted, but I was very angry with him (and with our Ambassador in Baghdad, who had attempted to have the Shah arrested when he landed in Iraq). My brother had told me that when he arrived in Rome, our Ambassador had conveniently taken a holiday, and left instructions that the Shah was not to be given the keys to his own personal car, which had been left at the Embassy. I know it is human nature to change sides when your side seems to be defeated, and I can even understand why the Iranians, after centuries of invasion and infiltration, have become very adaptable in their political loyalties. But I still find it hard to accept the speed and the facility with which so many of my brother's friends and allies joined the opposition whenever he was in trouble.

After the tensions and pressures of the previous two years I thought I would be going home now, but that was not to happen as I had planned. One day shortly after I had returned to Paris, I accompanied a friend and her son to their doctor's office. While I was there, I happened to mention that I had been under a great deal of stress and that I had not been feeling as well as usual.

"Why don't you let me look you over while you're here?" the doctor suggested.

I agreed, but I became uneasy as his manner grew quieter and more serious during the examination. His diagnosis: tuberculosis. "Not an advanced case, young woman, and for that you can be grateful. With the drugs that are available today, you should be back on your feet in six months. But I think you can begin treatment at once."

So at a time when I had hoped to be flying back to Teheran, I found myself headed for a private sanitorium in the Swiss village of Arosa. The doctor told me that I had been suffering from the disease for perhaps a year—a year when I had been so preoccupied with my brother's political problems, with my son's illness, and with my new relationship with Mehdi that I had been completely detached from what was happening within my own body. It was only after I knew that my brother was securely reestablished on his throne that I allowed myself the "luxury" of being ill.

The months at Arosa passed slowly, but my mood was basically optimistic. Since I had no other outlet for the nervous energy that always keeps me busy and active, I focused all determination and will on getting well (with the help of a very effective course of drug therapy). To pass the time, I read—detective novels and light fiction in English and French—listened to music and looked forward to the visits of friends. (Mehdi was only able to visit a few times, and I was allowed only one furlough to Paris.) The loneliness and the forced inactivity were the most difficult aspects of my illness. (To this day it is hard for me to cope with solitude for more than an hour or so at a time; I think solitude evokes for me some of the painful memories of my childhood.)

Also, of course, I felt a certain frustration at not being able to observe and share what must have been one of the most joyous months of my brother's reign. (It has become so fashionable to criticize the Pahlavis and to portray the Shah as an autocratic despot that people forget how well-loved he

145

was for so many years.) As I always do when I am away from home, I followed the news from Iran on the radio, in newspapers and magazines, and through reports from friends. I was not surprised to learn that my brother had behaved with restraint toward Mossadegh, a man who had tried to destroy him. In his 37-year reign the Shah has never responded with vindictiveness or anger toward those who plotted against him or tried to take his life. I think he fatalistically accepts the fact that these risks come with the Crown.

After Mossadegh's coup was exposed, the Iranian people turned violently against him, and he was in danger of losing his life at the hands of lynch mobs that cried for his death. My brother ordered one of his trusted friends to hide Mossadegh until order was restored and the former Prime Minister could be brought to trial.

If Mossadegh's crime had been a simple assassination plot, I think my brother would have pardoned him and sent him into exile. But since the crime was one of attempting to overthrow the legitimate government of Iran, he called for a trial. And a very dramatic trial it was, orchestrated by the defendant in his pajamas and dressing gown, complete with five-hour Mossadegh orations, fainting spells, hunger strikes, and curses against the judge, the defense attorney, the prosecution, and the Shah. At the end, Mossadegh was found guilty and sentenced to three years in prison, but the Shah intervened and commuted the sentence to one and a half years. After his release Mossadegh retired to his house in the country, where he lived until his death of throat cancer in 1966.

Once the trial was over, Iran experienced an atmosphere of calm, during which Prime Minister Zahedi worked to restore order out of disorder. Since Zahedi's first priority was to start Iran's oil moving again, there was no choice but to reestablish diplomatic relations with the British and to open negotiations with an international consortium of British, American, French, and Dutch oil companies. In September 1954 a 50–50 agreement was drawn up, and in 1958 the terms were changed to 75–25, which gave Iran a larger share of the profits.

To help Iran out of its virtually bankrupt state, President Eisenhower's administration granted $45 million in emergency aid, so that when I returned home from Arosa, it was to a country that was again, as it had been under my father, in the midst of a political and economic regeneration.

147

## · VII ·

# "THE ITINERANT AMBASSADOR"

The post-Mossadegh years were transitional years for both my brother and me. The Shah emerged from this crisis feeling that this was a time for strong direction from the throne, that Iran lacked the political maturity and the experience (let us not forget that the vast majority of our people were still illiterate) to operate effectively under any imitation of a Western-style democracy or of English parliamentarianism. Like my father, he wanted to see Iran move out of its underdeveloped status, to realize some of the economic and social potential we all knew was there. He made the judgment that for the long term, Iran's interests would be best served if he very firmly took the reins of government in his own hands and then gradually relinquished this power as our political system developed the maturity, strength, and flexibility to accommodate both democratic principles and the Iranian national character.

My brother was able to do this because our people were feeling a certain weariness and revulsion after the social disorder and economic upheaval of Mossadegh's regime.

149

Ironically, Mossadegh himself had served to crystallize and organize our people's resentment and frustration, which had come from the social and economic miseries of the war and postwar period. Now they were tired and spent and ready for a "father figure" who would take charge of the country's problems (and their problems) and solve them.

Iran's government would become more and more the Shah's government and this would remain the case until the last years of his regime. This turning point would have critical repercussions, not during the late Fifties and early Sixties, when the Shah was still riding an enormous wave of popularity, but later. In taking the personal leadership over Iran's destiny, though, my brother in a sense set a time bomb which would eventually go off when enough factions, within our country and outside, decided that he was not solving our problems quickly enough—or on the other hand that he was solving them too quickly.

One of the decisions taken at this time, one that would become the *bête noire* of my brother's regime, was the creation of an Iranian secret police, the SAVAK. Although some of the harshest and often most distorted allegations concerning this organization would later appear in the American press, SAVAK was in fact a cooperative effort with our American friends. Its operatives were trained by the CIA, with some assistance from MOSAD, the Israeli secret police. Its main function was to help the Shah hold the line against Communist infiltration—a strong and ever-present danger in Iran for decades. In fact, the first investigation conducted by Teymur Bakhtiar, the first chief of SAVAK, uncovered a ring of Communist infiltrators in the army, which, undetected, might well have succeeded in introducing a leftist government by military coup.

Although this organization was to have an ominous public image in later years, I believe that it was no better and no worse than any nation's counterintelligence or secret police, whether it be Israel's MOSAD or the French SDECE, or the British MI6. SAVAK was meant to keep the Shah abreast of any political opposition within the country; it was not his wish to create, as some have said, a kind of GULAG atmosphere or a security force of yes-men. On the contrary, my brother always made the distinction between political nihilism and constructive disagreement and dissent. And while, for example, he was keenly alert to the dangers of Russian-directed Communist infiltration, he actively tried to integrate leftist Iranian intellectuals into the Government, and in the course of his reign, many of these held high posts.

As my brother became stronger, I retired from active participation in domestic politics. My brother no longer needed my help in this area, and clearly I was temperamentally unsuited for political game-playing. My bluntness and my lack of patience often got me in trouble, and the way in which fickle politicians "blow with the wind" made me angry and cynical. I decided to concentrate for the moment on social issues and welfare projects (and God knows there was a great deal that needed to be done) and to put my own personal house, both literally and figuratively, in order.

My house on Kakh Avenue had been sold while I was away in Arosa. Now, and until the 1979 revolution, I would live in the Saadabad complex, in a house I loved because it was built from a sketch made by my brother. In later years (especially after Iran's oil-prosperity created many millionaires who built elaborate villas and castles) my friends and associates would suggest that I renovate and enlarge the Saadabad house. But somehow I never had the heart to change it or an interest in making it grander.

After my exile and my long illness I think I was so happy to be in Iran and close to my brother again that my new house seemed fine as it was, and as warm and welcoming as any place I had ever been. Before I left France, I reached an understanding with Mehdi: I would ask Shafiq for a divorce and we would marry as soon as possible. When I spoke to Shafiq about ending our marriage, he agreed to a quiet divorce—provided I would wait a few years, until our children were older. I agreed. I have never been a conventional mother—just as I have never been a conventional wife—but I have nevertheless had an uncommonly close and tender relationship with my children.

Since I felt that I was the partner who had failed to give the marriage the nurturing and attention that any marriage needs to thrive, I conceded that Shafiq might be right when he said that a divorce would be less disruptive to the children if it were postponed. The delay was difficult, but I think I had come to understand that there was a price for the public life I had chosen: if I could give very little of myself to my personal life, then I had to accept the fact that my greatest satisfactions would come from my work, that I would have brief and limited periods of personal happiness.

A few months after I returned to Iran, Mehdi followed. I explained to him that we would have to wait at least several years before we could be married, and he, remarkable and understanding man that he is, agreed. Since Teheran wasn't Paris, we could see and speak to each other only very discreetly—at large receptions and family gatherings at which my husband would not be present. I had been the subject of enough gossip—already my name had been romantically linked with almost every politician I had ever worked with, including the late prime ministers Hajir and Razmara—so that now, when there was a man I was truly interested in, I felt I should be careful. My brother had given his permission for a divorce, but I didn't want to cause him any additional embarrassment; a second divorce by a female member of the Royal Family would cause enough talk. It was enough for me—actually it had to be enough—to know that Mehdi was there and that he would be there when I was free to remarry.

The only men who have really dominated my life have been my father and my brother. But Mehdi has been, in his gentle and undemanding way, an important part of my life almost since the first days we met. In Paris he gave me the chance to be young and foolish and frivolous—a time I will never forget, especially since I had gone so quickly from a rather lonely childhood to an equally lonely marriage. And he was so generous and warm in his total approval of me that through his eyes I was able to see myself in a different light. For example, I had never liked what I saw in the mirror, even though men had told me I was attractive. I always wished for someone else's face (I don't know whose exactly), fairer skin, and more height. I always imagined that there were so few people in this world shorter than I that when I did see someone smaller, I felt a little bit of satisfaction. Mehdi told me I was perfect, and because he was my best friend, he made me see myself with fewer imperfections.

I have often landed in "hot water" because I usually say exactly what I am thinking, but Mehdi expressed delight with my bluntness. "You're not like other women," he would say. "There aren't any twists and turns between what goes on in your head and what comes out of your mouth. I like that." And because we were friends, I felt there was at least one person who would never be upset if I didn't think before I spoke.

Perhaps it was appropriate that I began a long and active period of working for women's rights in my country at a time when I had my keenest appreciation of being a woman. I confess that even though since childhood I had paid a price for being a woman, in terms of my education and personal freedom, I had not given much thought to the specific ways in which women in general were more oppressed than men, nor had I considered the theories behind this oppression. I had simply decided to live my life as I saw fit, take the defeats when they came and then move on. I assumed that I had gotten away with this attitude because I was a princess and the twin sister of the Shah.

Of course we had the seeds of a women's movement since the days of the constitutionalists, when a handful of

153

enlightened and courageous women joined with men in their political struggle against the Qajars. If we take a broad historical perspective, we can say that that isolated burst of activity had its roots in our ancient past. Before the Arab invasion of the mid-seventh century A.D., Iran had had two reigning queens, and our women had a broad range of rights and privileges, some of which are still under debate today. But after the Islamic conquests, Iran's women lost social status and civil rights, not as a result of Islam itself, but because of practices adopted under Arab influence. Once lost, these rights were not so easily regained (I hope this lesson will be noted by Iran's women today).

Throughout the first half of the twentieth century the reemergence of our women was slow. At the time I began my work for women's rights, we had a few scattered women's organizations, working at random, without any long-range goals or purpose. Their members did charity work on a volunteer basis, but they did not involve themselves in the fundamental issues of economic and political equality for women.

I made my first contact with some of these groups when I was looking for help in launching welfare projects. Later I met with representatives of various organizations to create a framework for our women's movement. Out of these meetings came a federation known as the High Council of Women's Organizations (later we became known as the Women's Organization of Iran) with a set of by-laws and a volunteer staff, over which I presided.

Our principal aim was to integrate Iranian women into every facet of society and to recreate the condition of equality our female ancestors had enjoyed centuries ago. Specifically, we worked for economic equality through vocational training; an awareness of civil rights and responsibilities through literacy classes and consciousness-raising meetings; international contact and a better understanding with women of other countries. In the last few years, when our membership had grown to almost a million women, with 400 branch organizations and a volunteer staff of 70,000, we initiated more direct political activity (such as the endorsement of parliamentary candidates).

This did not happen overnight. The work I am describing went on for the better part of two decades. Yet, if I may jump ahead, I can report that after the International Women's Year conference in Mexico in 1975, Iran was one of the first countries to draw up and implement a concrete "plan of action" stating that volunteer work could take women only so far, that we needed a full commitment from our government if women were to advance beyond the few traditional areas open to them, such as teaching and domestic service. We did get such a commitment from the Shah, and up until the revolution we met regularly with individual ministers and the full cabinet for ongoing discussions on how to increase and improve female participation in various areas of Iranian life.

On the political front, one of our proudest achievements was the passage of the Family Protection Act in 1975. This act gave Iran's women the most sweeping civil rights in the Islamic Middle East. It recognized a wife as an equal partner in marriage: in decision making, in planning the future of children, in divorce, and in the matter of child custody. It limited a man to one wife (indirectly, since the Koran permits as many as four) by laying down strict conditions which virtually made it impossible for him to marry a second time: the prospective polygamist had to have his first wife agree; had to have the financial means to support equal households; had to prove that his first wife was sterile or incurably ill. The act provided that a woman could seek divorce on the same grounds open to a man (these grounds were now clearly defined), and it created a machinery whereby she could seek, and collect, alimony and child support. In the event of her husband's death, the guardianship of children would be awarded to the wife;

155

previously all her male in-laws would have been given precedence.

To get these laws passed was an uphill fight all the way. Our various committees labored for hundreds of hours to word these provisions in such a way as to minimize both secular and religious resistance. We enlisted the cooperation of various ministers, since it was obvious to me that you cannot emancipate women in a male-dominated society without the active support of at least some of those men, and we sought the endorsement of Iran's more progressive mullahs (to whom we always prefaced our appeals with such remarks as; "Well, of course we understand that a woman's primary responsibility is to her husband and her children, but...").

Of course there were compromises at almost every step we took. For example, we wanted to put an end to the civil code provision that a woman could not hold a job without her husband's consent. "But just a moment," said one of the ministers at our meeting, "suppose my wife should decide to take a job that is not in keeping with my dignity."

"I'm afraid you'll have to give me an example," I said.

"Well, suppose she takes a job in a factory, or singing in a nightclub?"

"Are you saying those jobs are less honorable than the one you hold?"

Actually I realized even while we were talking that if this fairly enlightened man was raising an objection, then certainly the less progressive gentlemen in our midst would balk at a law allowing a wife unlimited job options. So we added a clause "protecting" a man's dignity—but at the same time we insisted that the clause be reciprocal and apply equally to men's jobs and women's dignity.

When it was finished, I said to my co-workers: "Do you realize that we have won something of a victory with this compromise? This is the first time that Iranian law has even recognized that Iranian women have any dignity, let alone agreed to 'protect' it."

By the time of the revolution we had almost complete equality with men, at least in the eyes of the law. We had even managed to allow abortion—indirectly, since our religion would not allow us to do it any other way—by decriminalizing it and by setting up medical guidelines under which it could be performed.

There were three more areas that still needed work: one was the law governing inheritance, the second was the law that required a wife to obtain her husband's permission whenever she wanted to travel outside the country. Resistance to change here came from a fear that we would have a rash of "runaway wives," though I argued long and hard that it was much more important to guard against "runaway husbands," who were, in most families, the major breadwinners. The final item on our agenda was the elimination of Article 179 of the penal code, which allowed a man to escape punishment if he killed his wife in a situation where he *believed* she had been guilty of adultery. This law had been so liberally interpreted in the past that a brother had once escaped sentencing for killing his sister—because he saw her getting into a taxi with a man.

Although implementing our reforms was by no means an easy task, we had many satisfactions. There was the day a minister friend of mine came to me and complained that women's rights had gone too far in Iran, because he was having a very hard time getting a divorce from his wife. "I'm very sorry if anything I've done has caused you problems," I said. "But I can't really say that I'm sorry the day is past when a man can discard a wife simply because he feels like it."

We had come such a long way since the days when Iran's women were almost invisible that it was hard for me to comprehend how women can relinquish those rights now with so little resistance. When I am optimistic, I think that the women of Iran have gone underground and are just waiting for an opportunity to surface and reassert themselves. In pessimistic moods, however, I think that perhaps our women have taken their freedom too lightly because they have not had to fight for it or go to jail for it, and that they will not realize how much they have lost until they have been effectively repressed again.

This period of expanded rights for women, of more education for more people, of broad programs of social welfare, was also marked by a turning point in Iran's foreign policy. For the first time since the war, we made a firm decision to form an alliance with the United States at the expense of Russia, a decision that colored the entire history of our country for decades and ultimately paved the way for the recent revolution.

In 1959 the Russians were again determined to make Iran an ally and thereby assert their influence over us. They even conceded to a nonaggression treaty and had convinced the Shah to sign it. But when the news of this Soviet alliance reached America, President Eisenhower sent my brother the promise of increased U.S. aid if he rejected the treaty.

So, when the Russian delegation came to Teheran to prepare a draft, my brother sent them home empty-handed, thus provoking the Russians to strong public denunciations of the Shah. In a press conference, Khrushchev said: "He will not succeed through pacts with the United States to save his rotten throne. He treated us as if we were Luxembourg, and he will be sorry." A *Pravda* article reinforced Khrushchev's threat, with the prophecy that, "The Shah's two-faced dealings will earn him the same fate as Iraq's King Faisal."

After a steady barrage of Russian attacks (and with the certain knowledge that the Soviets would not let up in their push to establish a presence in Iran, one way or another), we felt more than a little reassured by the visit Eisenhower made to Iran late in 1959, right after his trip to India. The U.S. President addressed the Parliament and praised the Shah, saying, "You have borne the force of powerful propaganda," and promising continued American support. (One could believe Eisenhower, too. When I visited him in the White House in 1956, I found him to be a practical and honest man, a humane person who could be trusted. Even though he had been ill and looked thin and weak, he told me he was determined to recover and run for reelection, which he did.)

The *Pravda* reference to King Faisal was, incidentally, a shrewdly chosen thrust, for Iraq's late king had been a very close family friend as well as an ally, and his death had touched us deeply. Faisal had been a charming young man, with a British education and a British gentleman's manner. He had been essentially a symbolic monarch, as the real power in Iraq was Prime Minister Nuri al-Said, a man who had built for Iraq the finest governmental machinery in the Middle East.

Since our families, as well as our countries, were very close (there were many friendly visits between Teheran and Baghdad), Faisal made a formal request to marry my niece Shahnaz. My brother left the choice to his daughter, and it was arranged that she and Faisal would meet in London in order to become better acquainted. After the meeting, Shahnaz said no to Faisal's proposal—which in my day was something a woman was not able to do.

Although in the summer of 1957, Faisal found another woman to marry, Princess Fazilat, a descendant of the Ottoman kings, the wedding never took place. On the evening of July 14, 1958, two Iraqi generals, Abd al-Karim Qassem and Abd al-Salam Aref, executed a coup in which King Faisal and his entire family tragically were massacred along with the Prime Minister, Nuri al-Said. We heard this news in Teheran with a deep sense of personal loss.

We watched with apprehension as our neighbor to the

west became a country beset by coups and assassinations. During the final years of Faisal's reign, in 1955, we had joined the Baghdad Pact (initiated by John Foster Dulles), which was to serve as a collective defense system for the participants (Iran, Iraq, Turkey, and Pakistan). Faisal's death put an end to the treaty.

Abd al-Karim Qassem succeeded Faisal, but he too, was assassinated in five years; so was his successor, Abd al-Salam Aref, who died in a mysterious helicoptor accident. As a result, Iraq's governing Revolutionary Committee was in a constant state of terror. Before each session, they searched one another for arms and took an oath not to kill one another—at least during the course of the meeting. (Only in the past decade, under the leadership of Hassan al-Bakr and Saddam Hussein, has Iraq enjoyed a stable government. Under Saddam Hussein, whom I met three years ago in Baghdad, relations between Iraq and Iran—which had been strained since the death of Faisal—were normalized.)

Whenever I see political situations like this, and like the recent events in my country, I am convinced that politics, and especially Middle Eastern politics, rarely manage to accommodate the principles of logic or friendship. Whenever I feel this cynical, I remember a fable based on La Fontaine that was often told by our Ambassador in Baghdad: "A scorpion was standing on the bank of a river, trying to think of a way to cross, when he saw a turtle. 'Can you help me cross the river?' he asked.

" 'Of course,' answered the turtle. 'Climb on my back and I will give you a ride.'

"As they reached the halfway mark in the river, the scorpion started to sting the turtle on the shell. 'What are you doing?' asked the turtle. 'I'm trying to help you. Is this the way you pay me for my assistance? And you are wasting your energy—you can't sting me through my shell. Why are you doing this?'

" 'Oh, be quiet,' said the scorpion. 'Don't ask me why. Don't you know we are in the Middle East?'"

Although my brother had loved Soraya very deeply, their marriage suffered serious strain when years passed and they were unable to have children. The strain increased after 1954, when my brother Ali Reza died and there was no male heir left to succeed the Shah.

Soraya consulted many specialists in Europe and the United States, but without any results. There was a great deal of speculation about alternate solutions to this dilemma, such as the possibility of changing the line of succession or the possibility of the Shah's taking a second wife, but none of these was seriously considered. Soraya and the Shah sadly came to the conclusion that there was nothing for them to do but divorce. One evening, in March 1958, we were all invited to a party at the palace; none of us had been told, but this was to be the last evening Soraya and the Shah would spend together. The party was very lively and very festive on the surface; certainly none of the guests could know how sad the host and hostess felt.

The following morning Soraya flew out of Teheran to Switzerland and it was officially announced that there was another royal divorce. My brother conferred on Soraya the title of "Royal Princess," and although the marriage had to end, I think it was with a great deal of regret and mutual concern.

When, twenty years later, my brother was receiving cancer treatment in a New York hospital, Soraya was one of the first to send a cable. We had never been good friends, but I was so touched by her gesture that I wished I could have given her a warm hug there and then.

Although my brother wasn't really anxious to find another wife, the pressure that had precipitated the divorce—the need for an heir to the throne—mounted even

161

more. Once again, the round of discreet inquiries began. This time it was the court dentist, Esfandiar Diba, who initiated the matchmaking process when he told Ardeshir Zahedi (who had married Shahnaz and was now the Shah's son-in-law) that he had a lovely niece, Farah, who would make an ideal wife for the Shah.

Farah Diba's father, who died when she was ten years old, was from Tabriz; her mother was from the province of Gilan. Farah had been educated first in Teheran private schools and later at École Spéciale d'Architecture in Paris. Indeed she remembers meeting the Shah once during her school years in Paris when he attended a reception for Iranian students.

Ardeshir Zahedi spoke to the Shah about this young woman, who was intelligent, articulate, well-educated, and very attractive. Since Farah was in Teheran for her summer holidays, a meeting was arranged by Ardeshir and Shahnaz. This was the first time that the Shah had seen a prospective bride in person without the usual preliminary look at photographs. A week later my brother proposed.

Farah made a trip to Paris to buy her trousseau, and when she returned, the engagement was announced. On December 21, 1959, my brother and Farah were married at the Golestan Palace, with some 400 guests in attendance.

Whenever I try to describe my sister-in-law, I find myself thinking in superlatives. Although Farah Diba was 21 when she married my brother, and hadn't known anything but the life of a student, she assumed her royal duties as if she had been born to them. She has been a perfect wife and an attentive mother. Ten months after their marriage, my brother and his wife had a son and heir, Crown Prince Cyrus Reza. Later there would be three more children: Farahnaz, born in 1963; Ali Reza, 1966; and Leila, 1970.

With her love for the arts, Queen Farah played a major role in Iran's cultural revival (she was also active in social welfare causes). She established the Arts Festival of Shiraz-Persepolis, presided over the International Film Festival, and actively sponsored the careers of many Iranian artists. Her personal touch, as well as her architectural talent, are very much in evidence in the house she designed for herself and my brother and which stands near the Niavaran Palace.

After my brother's marriage to Farah, our family's social life fell into a fairly regular routine. Twice a week we would visit my mother; twice a week the family would visit me; once a week Shams would receive us; and once a week, if there was no official function scheduled, we would spend the evening with the Shah and Farah. Each of us would include some personal friends in these gatherings but basically they were quiet visits, passed in conversation or in playing bridge. My sister Shams, whose first marriage had ended in divorce, was now married to the director of the Department of Culture and Art, so at her house we might enjoy some sort of musicale or perhaps a performance by some folk singers or dancers. On a warm summer evening my brother and I might sit in the garden and enjoy the delightfully cool, dry air of the mountains.

My brother was always very formal, even during these relatively relaxed visits. I don't think I ever saw him with his tie loosened or his jacket unbuttoned. Like my father, he never overindulged at dinner, and he permitted himself only one cigarette after each meal. With his women guests, my brother was always very gallant, and unlike many Iranian men, he extended every courtesy to his wife. One evening, for example, when Farah was late for dinner, the Shah insisted that everyone wait for her (most Iranian men would have gone ahead without their wives).

After my brother's remarriage I began to think of my own marriage to Mehdi. Once again I spoke to Shafiq about a divorce, and this time he agreed. Ours had not been a love match, and perhaps that is why we were able to part in a calm and relatively amicable manner.

Shafiq married again, but we remained friends, and we often talked about matters concerning the children and each other. A few years ago, when Shafiq learned he had cancer, I was the first person he told, and together we tried to think of how to break the news to the children. When he died some time later, I shared the grief my children felt over the loss of their father.

Seven years elapsed between the time Shafiq and I first discussed ending our marriage and the time we actually did so. Our children were now 15 and 9, but they were still upset and angry about the divorce. My son Shahriar said he wanted to live with his father, and my daughter at first said that was her choice too. Although I loved my children dearly, I didn't try to persuade them to stay with me; I think I felt that I could not be a "total mother" any more than I had been able to be a "total wife." But after Azadeh had lived with her father a few months, she said to me: "Mummy, I want to come home now. I want to live with you."

"Are you sure, Azadeh? Are you really sure?" I asked. "Your father loves you very much, too." As happy as Azadeh had made me by wanting to come home, I knew Shafiq could probably give her more time and personal attention. My own childhood had been so solitary and so lonely that I didn't want any of my children ever to feel unwanted or unloved. I never wanted them to be afraid of me, as I had been afraid of my father, and so I encouraged them always to speak frankly to me, to tell me exactly what they thought or felt, regardless of what my reaction might be.

Azadeh was very much like me—even as a child she was strong-willed and outspoken—and when she decided to live with me, the subject was closed as far as she was concerned. We have often been physically separated, as I told her we might be, and when she was 13 she went to school in France, but we have somehow evolved a close emotional relationship, more like two friends than mother and daughter. Even now we talk on the telephone almost every day.

The rift with Shahriar took a little longer to heal, but as he began to plan for his own future and to put childhood behind him, I think he became a bit more tolerant of adult failures and mistakes. Shahriar was very much like my brother Ali Reza, a born military man. He had hoped to become a pilot, but since he was nearsighted, he settled instead on a navy career. At the age of 16 he enrolled in the Britannia Royal Naval College in Dartmouth, England.

My son from my first marriage, Shahram, had finished school at Le Rosey and was now studying at Harvard, preparing for a career in business. When I looked at my children, seeing them in my mind as little babies and seeing them as they were, I felt as if the years had raced by, as if I had lived through a series of cycles. Sometimes I had learned from my mistakes, often I had not—and here I was getting ready to marry again. I was 40 years old, and this was the first time I was marrying for love; but I was still a woman who could not live a life that revolved around a man. Mehdi said he could accept this, and we both agreed that we would try never to impose our individual wishes on each other. But with two broken marriages behind me—for whatever reason—I began my new marriage with mixed emotions: anticipation and doubt.

For our wedding, Mehdi and I flew to Paris, the city where we had met. The trip wasn't really a sentimental or an extravagant one—since it wasn't exactly customary or accepted for a royal princess to have three marriages, I didn't want to draw any more attention to myself than was absolutely necessary. I was married very quietly in June 1960 in a pink pleated chiffon dress, at the Iranian Embassy in Paris, to a man who was as near-perfect a human being as I have ever known. Our relationship might change in the years to come, but my opinion of him would never change.

We honeymooned in the south of France, at my house in Juan les Pins, one of my favorite retreats for enjoying the sun and "getting away from it all." I am reminded that it was at Juan les Pins that I had met Jacqueline and John Kennedy. It was the summer before, and a friend had invited Mehdi and me to lunch. When we arrived we found that there were two other guests—Senator and Mrs. Kennedy. Mehdi had gone to school with Mrs. Kennedy's sister Lee, and when he was introduced to Jacqueline, he asked about her sister and reminisced about his school days in Paris.

No matter what the rumors were about the discord in their private lives, the Kennedys then appeared to be a golden couple—attractive, happy, and self-assured. While Mehdi and Jackie talked in French, I said to Jack: "I hear that you will be President soon. Is this prediction true?" He laughed and said: "Well, you know that the presidency is the ultimate goal of any ambitious politician. I think I have the will and the potential to reach that goal, and once I'm there I believe I can serve my country well." Then he turned his head toward Jackie and added; "You must agree that I have a beautiful and charming wife who would make a great first lady." After lunch Mehdi said: "This man is going to go very far in American politics," and I was inclined to agree with him.

Although many of my brother's programs altered the quality of life in Iran, I think the most significant one was the land reform he initiated in 1963 as part of his White Revolution. Through a series of sweeping changes, the Shah undertook to transform Iran into a modern state in which more of its citizens shared.

Almost three-fourths of Iran's population was engaged in some form of agriculture, but more than a third of the country's land under cultivation was owned by a small number of landed families comprising less than one percent of the population. To make these numbers more equitable, the Shah distributed his own lands in 1950, and over the next 15 years he tried systematically to reapportion public and private lands by limiting the number of acres a single landowner might hold. In the early stages of this program almost 500 million acres were distributed among 42,000 farmers. By the final phase, land had been apportioned to

166

some 2 million small farmers, and more than 2,800 farming cooperatives had been created and had distributed over 20,000 million rials in agricultural loans.

All of this was not accomplished without a great deal of resistance, both from the landed gentry (who were in many cases politicians) and from the clergy (who were often the custodians of large estates, as the Catholic clergy had been in Europe centuries ago). When in 1963 a law limiting individual ownership of lands was submitted to a plebiscite, we saw a wave of bloody riots, fires, and acts of sabotage.

Incidentally, the man behind these disturbances was a mullah named Ruhollah Khomeini, who opposed all of my brother's modernization programs, but especially those dealing with land reform and the emancipation of women. When he was apprehended, another clergyman, Ayatollah Kazem Shariat Madari (now Khomeini's strongest rival), interceded on his behalf with General Hassan Pakravan of SAVAK, pleading that Khomeini be given the designation of "ayatollah," which would give him immunity from the most severe penalties under the law for his treasonous activities. This was done, and Khomeini was merely asked to leave the country. (When Khomeini took power in 1979, he repaid his benefactor, General Pakravan, by having him executed, thus conveniently eliminating the man who knew that Khomeini himself had had ties in the past to SAVAK.)

In addition to land reform, the White Revolution called for nationalization of forests; the sale of government industries to cooperatives and private individuals; the establishment of a profit-sharing system between management and labor within these industries; revisions of the electoral laws to provide for universal (particularly female) suffrage; the creation of a Corps of Literacy, a Corps of Health, and a Corps of Development, which would improve the quality of education, medical/dental care, and agriculture throughout the country; the establishment of "Houses of Justice" — village tribunals—to simplify the judicial system and make it accessible to all; a plan for urban and rural reconstruction; nationalization of water resources; reorganization of the government bureaucracy; and an overhaul of the educational system.

Naturally there is always a gap between the conceptualization of ambitious development programs and their realization. Today when I hear attacks on my brother for what he failed to accomplish, with little mention of what he did in fact achieve, I wonder if these attacks are not the work of those who, for personal reasons, did not want to see Iran moving so quickly from its underdeveloped have-not status to a thriving—and assertive—state.

In the "boom" decade following the White Revolution, Iran passed through dramatic and dizzying changes. Our transport-communication system was radically improved, with over 20,000 miles of new roads, 17 airports, and a telephone network that reached most of the country. With 14 dams that irrigated a quarter million acres of land, Iran's electric power increased tenfold.

Realizing that the country's oil reserves would be depleted by the beginning of the twenty-first century, the Shah initiated research into alternative sources of energy, particularly solar and nuclear energy, which he hoped would also power desalination plants to increase water resources. (By 1979, in fact, there were six nuclear energy plants under construction.) He believed that oil should be conserved for industrial use, so Iran moved very quickly into the production of petrochemicals, with plants in Shiraz, Shahpur, Abadan, and Kharg. In a country that had been almost totally agricultural, we saw the rapid development of industry—iron, sulfur, and steel (at the end of the Shah's regime, the iron and steel complex at Isfahan was projected to produce 4 million tons per year). Iran was exporting household appliances, automobiles, tractors, and buses to Europe and the Middle East. The production of electricity rose from 689 million kilowatt hours in 1960 to 18 billion kilowatt hours in 1979. Cement production increased elevenfold between 1962 and 1974, to 5 million tons per year.

In this economic climate we also saw a real estate boom, with the value of land multiplying hundreds of times over. Like many Iranians, I was able to increase my personal wealth through several real estate transactions, among them the development of a 1,000-villa housing project. In recent years I have seen many newspaper stories suggesting that members of the royal family became rich by dishonest or devious methods, but the truth is that in the rapidly growing economy we had, it was very possible to become wealthy by perfectly straightforward means; witness the bumper crop of new millionaires who had been simple shopkeepers or small businessmen. For anyone who already had any kind of a personal fortune, the opportunities were virtually limitless. In the years following my father's death, I had invested the major portion of my inheritance in unset gems, mainly Russian emeralds. These appreciated enormously over the years, as did my real estate holdings, giving me substantial capital to make other investments.

While domestic prosperity raised Iran to the rank of the ninth wealthiest country in the world, the Shah pursued a foreign policy that was balanced between our primary alliance with the United States and our good relations with almost all other countries.

Within the Middle East we had relatively stable, if not always cordial relations with our good neighbors. As the British phased out their military presence in the Persian Gulf area, my brother felt it was more imperative than ever for Iran to have a modern, well-equipped army. Our military buildup caused some concern to our Arab neighbors, although Iran certainly had no aggressive intentions toward them. The Shah's independent stance on oil did not always sit well with other OPEC members, particularly since he would not use oil as a political weapon against Israel (although Iran did not sell oil directly to Israel, the Shah placed no restrictions on the ultimate destination of any oil tankers once they left our ports; consequently Israel was able to buy Iranian oil).

We did have several dear and close friends in the capitals of the Middle East. Regardless of what was happening on the world political scene, we always had a friend in Jordan's King Hussein. The Western press sometimes refers to him as "the little king" because of his stature and the size of his country, but he is a most remarkable man and a courageous ruler. To Iran he has been like a brother. In addition to the usual state visits, we shared many purely social holidays together, either at the Caspian Sea or in Jordan. Hussein and my brother shared a common interest in sports, especially water and snow skiing and flying, and Queen Farah and the late Queen Alia got along very well. Since my brother's illness, Hussein's calls and personal messages have been a great comfort to us.

With Morocco's King Hassan we had not as much personal contact, but I did get to know him fairly well when he welcomed my brother for two months after the 1979 revolution. King Hassan generously received the Shah in the true tradition of Oriental hospitality, even though he created problems for himself in doing so.

Another good friend has been Egypt's Anwar Sadat. The world knows him now as the statesman he is, a leader who has risked all to end warfare and bloodshed. But beyond that, he is a religous man in the truest sense of the word, a man of rare integrity who will not sacrifice principle for expediency—a rare quality anywhere in the world today.

After Anwar Sadat became president of Egypt, one of his early priorities was to end the Russian presence in Egypt (and with it substantial Russian assistance). My brother offered President Sadat financial aid to help Egypt through that difficult period. Years later, when so few of my brother's former friends were willing even to acknowledge his existence, Anwar Sadat extended a welcoming hand—again, at great political and personal risk. Although the Shah was very grateful for the invitation to settle in Egypt, he did not want to add to a great man's already heavy burden.

Although Iran's relations with the British have been ambivalent over the years, the Shah has maintained cordial contact with the British Royal Family since the beginning of his reign. Over the years there have been many visits between the two families (in fact the Queen was expected in Teheran in December 1978, but the trip was cancelled because of the disturbances in the city). I have always found the Queen a gracious woman, and I am particularly fond of the Queen Mother, who is an intelligent and cheerful woman, buoyant in spite of her years, and blessed with a delightful and quick sense of humor. The last time I saw England it was to open the Ashraf Pahlavi Library, which I had donated to Wadham College at Oxford.

Of all the Western leaders I have met, I think the one I most admired, ever since the days of the French resistance, was Charles de Gaulle, a military leader who was almost fanatic in his patriotism. Whatever France is today, I think it owes to De Gaulle. He was a tall, stately man (we had to have a special bed for him when he first visited Teheran), soft-spoken, the quintessential diplomat, with always the appropriate word for any occasion.

My favorite De Gaulle story dates back to a state visit he made with Madame de Gaulle to Iran in October 1963. The first stop was a petrochemical plant which the French were building near Shiraz, and this of course involved the usual round of inspections and speeches. Next, the presidential party was driven to our ancient city of Persepolis, where they were greeted by the director of the museum. I think everyone in the party must have groaned inwardly as they all stood on the monumental steps of the museum in the blazing sun while the museum director began to read from a prepared speech that seemed to be 20 or 30 pages long; clearly the gentleman was conscientiously prepared to give

171

the entire history of the ancient city. As he read, "Late one evening, while he was very drunk, Alexander the Great took one of his mistresses on his shoulders and she set fire to this great building," the gentleman paused to turn the page. President de Gaulle spoke immediately: "Alors," he said, "let us go at once to see what remains!"

Toward my brother, De Gaulle displayed an almost paternal affection. Not long before he died, he said to the Shah, "I think you have accomplished many fine things in a very short time. But," he added, "I would advise you to be careful not to be outflanked by your right."

Yet for the most part I feel that Western leaders and diplomats have not shown much basic understanding of psychology and traditions other than their own. In America, there have been startling variations from administration to administration in the perception of cultures outside the Western hemisphere. With regard to Iranian internal affairs, for example, many American politicians have made serious mistakes in judgment because they persist in applying American concepts of "the way things should be" and American techniques for achieving their notion of this ideal condition. In their distaste for what they see as "authoritarian" leadership—along with their fear of growing Communist influence in the world—they have put their faith in politicians who more often than not have had only superficial solutions to these dangers. The results have often been disastrous (witness Dean Acheson's mistaken evaluation of Mossadegh as a bulwark against Communism and the State Department's first assessment of Khomeini).

Under President Kennedy's Administration, for example, my brother was pressured into appointing two "liberal" prime ministers: Ali Amini, who tried (like Mossadegh) to reduce the Shah to a symbolic monarch (the Shah replaced him with Asadollah Alam in 1962), and Ali Mansour, who was assassinated by a fanatical theological student in 1965.

Events and crises that the American system could

readily withstand and absorb would destroy an Iranian government or plunge the country into desperate confusion and disorder. A president like Harry Truman could dismiss a powerful and popular general like Douglas MacArthur with no more repercussions than a brief flurry of popular and press indignation. In Iran such a move would almost certainly have provoked a military coup. In America entire industries can go on strike, students can demonstrate, militants can attack the police, and still the country goes on, the government continues to function.

When the subject turns to "human rights," Americans have a remarkably limited interpretation, a readiness to point a finger at others who don't conform to their own interpretation, and a disregard for the fact that different cultures may have a different set of natural priorities.

When I came to the UN it was with this issue of human rights foremost on my mind. After my turbulent and rather disillusioning foray into the arena of domestic politics, I saw the UN in a very idealistic light. I felt as if I had arrived at the natural end of a long road, one I had traveled in my mind ever since I learned about discrimination on the streets of Johannesburg.

In my own country I had developed my own ideas about what the most fundamental human rights were: the right to food, shelter, clothing, work, medical care, and a basic education. In my own country these areas had been my principal concern. (I feel I must point out that by the final years of my brother's reign there was not a single child in Iran who did not have shoes or whose belly was distended with hunger.)

Now, in the UN, I felt I had found the natural forum for discussing and solving the problems that concerned me most. The first committee I worked with was the Human Rights Committee, and the first speech I made was on the subject of discrimination. I believed wholeheartedly that I had become part of a body that could make a difference.

Normally my day begins rather late (since I don't usually go to sleep until two or three in the morning), but here I got up early, had a quick breakfast, and started work with the 10:30 session.

For three months a year the delegates formed a small, closely knit community. Most of us lunched together in the delegates' dining room, then went back for the afternoon session, which ran until six o'clock. After a quick dinner— for me this is usually a hamburger or a small steak, some salad, and a Coca-Cola—it was time for the evening round of receptions. Although these could be glittering affairs, they were really an extension of the working day, with conversation focused mainly on current international subjects under discussion. It was at one of my own receptions, incidentally, that I introduced Shirley MacLaine to several of my Chinese friends. (I remember how drawn she was to them, and soon after that she made her first trip to China and wrote her book about it.)

While my primary concerns were hunger, illiteracy, and women's rights, I saw myself in a broader sense as a spokesperson for the Third World point of view. I have enjoyed the cosmopolitan atmosphere and the cultural advantages of the Western capitals, but I have always felt closer to the people of the Third World countries. As the citizen of a country that has experienced the problems of a have-not status and the dislocations and growing pains that come with sudden prosperity, I feel affinity with others who are struggling through similar problems. Their frustrations and needs and hopes seem much more immediate and pressing to me than do the concerns of more sophisticated and more intensely developed countries.

I felt very strongly, for example, that politically the UN should not be a reflection of the world political arena, with the big powers having the means to overrule the wishes of

*Visiting the Hermitage during one of my Russian trips*

*My son Shahram and my niece Shahnaz*

*The Shah distributing Crown lands to the people of Iran*

*Queen Elizabeth with the Shah at an official reception in Teheran*
*( in the background is General Fereydoun Jam, who was my first "fiance,"*
*but who subsequently married my sister Shams)*

*The Shah and Queen Farah visit President Charles de Gaulle and Madame de Gaulle in Paris*

*The Shah and Queen Farah with President John Kennedy and his wife, Jacqueline, at the White House*

*The Shah and President Lyndon B. Johnson in Washington*

*My son Shahram and my daughter Azadeh*

*The Shah and Crown Prince*
*Cyrus Reza*

*With my late son Shahriar on the*
*island of Hormoz*

*My husband Mehdi Bushehri and I during a 1962 trip to the Crimea (Russia)*

*At the U N with Secretary-General U Thant*

*Visiting a small village in Iran*

*Visiting a primary school*

*With Abram Sachar, President of Brandeis University*

*At Brandeis University, where Coretta King and I
received honorary doctorate degrees*

*At my Saadabad home with the President of the Republic of Senegal,
Léopold Senghor and his wife*

*Addressing the UN General Assembly*

*Visiting England's Queen Mother at her home*

*At a party with England's Princess Margaret, at the Iranian Embassy in London (1975)*

*With the Iranian delegation at the UN (Fereydoun Hoveyda standing behind me on the right)*

*Attending a women's conference in India (1977)*

*With a young Tibetan girl (1977)*

*At the "Poster Wall" of China (1977)*

*Visiting the people of Tibet (1977)*

*In China, with Chairman Hua Kuo-Feng and an interpreter (1977)*

*Visiting India's Prime Minister Moraji Desai*

*Presenting UN Secretary-General Kurt Waldheim with a check for
$2 million for the International Women's Year*

*With President Jimmy Carter and his wife, Rosalynn, Teheran New Year's
Eve party, 1977*

smaller nations at will. I believe that the veto power—an exclusive prerogative of the big nations—is wrong because one country could exercise its will against the voices of 140 smaller countries. And in all my years of attending countless sessions and meetings I came to feel the frustration of seeing resolutions that were passed (after tons of paperwork) come to nothing because they had only a lip-service kind of support from the major powers.

When the UN was not in session, I visited many other Third World countries, as a kind of unofficial, itinerant ambassador, to learn more about their people and their problems firsthand.

One country which held a certain fascination for me was Indonesia, which, with its 90 million people, was the world's largest Islamic nation. Indonesia's brand of Islam has a Buddhist flavor, and because it was brought there by merchant caravans from India, rather than by Arab conquests, it is a more relaxed, less fundamentalist form of religion than in Iran.

I first met President Sukarno, the man who governed Indonesia for more than twenty years, in 1965. He was a tall (by Indonesian standards), handsome man, an intelligent, very eloquent speaker. I was taken by his belief in an economic amalgam of communism and capitalism and in a form of government he liked to call "guided democracy".

Another country I visited, one I returned to over and over again was India, a remarkable and complex culture encompassing some 450 million people. I made my first trip shortly after the death of Mahatma Gandhi and after the partition of the country, at a time when there was still fighting between Hindus and Muslims.

I had imagined that this would be a flat, tropical country, but what I found was a cruel land, from the peaks of the Himalayas to the heart of Asia, steaming jungles to the

Indian Ocean—a country where monsoons bring torrents of rain that kill thousands.

I saw a stunning mixture of past and present in this country where 14 principal languages and 300 dialects are spoken. I saw factories and many examples of advanced industries. India's engineers were building jets, ships, and locomotives. But the faces of the people, their clothes, and their gestures—these bore an uncanny resemblance to the statues and paintings I saw in the temples.

Although there was so much poverty and hunger everywhere, I met millionaires who devoted their money and energy to building shelters for ailing sacred cows or to the feeding of ants. Human life seemed so vulnerable and frail, but in the bazaars I saw cows roaming at will, eating whatever they wished; when we approached one of these animals in an automobile, we could not even sound the horn.

When I met Prime Minister Jawaharlal Nehru for the first time, he was, at 70, still a handsome, energetic man who worked 17 hours a day. We traveled together to Kashmir (crossing the snow-covered Himalayas, which reminded me so much of the Swiss landscape), discussing the problems of our respective countries. Nehru was an articulate politician, a socialist who disliked capitalism, an agnostic who had become a philosopher during the ten years he spent in a British jail.

He felt that if India failed to make very rapid economic progress, it would inevitably turn Communist, and he spoke of his frustrations in trying to direct such progress. "Every other day is a holiday in this country," he said. "It's a wonder we get anything done. For myself, I have stopped taking any time off at all. And the people here—how can I push them ahead while they still adore cows?"

In his foreign policy he advocated an approach he described as "active neutrality," and he criticized the Americans for their assistance to Pakistan and their backing of Franco and Chiang Kai-shek. Like me, he was in favor of admitting the Chinese to the UN. He declared that China was India's friend, so the Chinese attack was a great personal blow to him, one that made a wreckage of his career.

When I saw him again in 1964, after this attack, he seemed morally and physically diminished. After I returned to Teheran, I said to my brother, "This Nehru I have seen will not live very long." Three months later he died.

I established and maintained personal contact with his successor, Indira Gandhi. I think she was very much her own person—tough, shrewd, and independent. The one notable influence of her father, who disliked fat people, was that she was always on a strict diet.

History hasn't often seen a woman guide the destiny of so many millions, and I followed the career of this extraordinary leader with interest. She had, I believe, a lonely childhood, since her grandfather, her mother, and her father were often in prison. With such a background it was almost inevitable that she became a political person early in life. At boarding school in Switzerland she participated in political demonstrations, and later as a student at Oxford she joined the Labor Party. When she was jailed for her political views, she would try to make her imprisonment productive by lecturing her cellmates. Since she was well informed in many areas—art and literature, as well as politics—she was very helpful to her father when he was India's Minister of Information.

When she came into power, she was the darling of the intellectual left, as Mrs. Roosevelt had been in the United States. When she and I discussed feminist issues, she would say; "I'm not a feminist—I am a human being." But unquestionably Indian feminists made enormous strides under her regime, as reflected by the presence of 59 women in the country's parliament. During her first administration, she was officially cool toward Iran (my brother and I both tried to improve relations) because of our friendship with Pakistan.

These ties to Pakistan were closest when my friendship with Zulikfar Ali Bhutto started in 1964; he was then Foreign Minister under Ayub Khan. There were many visits between our two capitals. I remember in particular a banquet he gave for me. While I have no problems talking to individuals in any walk of life, I tend to get stage fright when I have to make a formal speech before a group. On this evening I had a blinding headache, and as I got up to speak, I was afraid I was going to faint. Ali Bhutto came to my assistance, holding my speech for me and steadying my shoulders so I could read it.

The last time I saw him, he was complaining about U.S. intervention in his country. When Pakistan wanted to buy a nuclear plant from France, there had been some demonstrations and riots. "I know the Americans are behind this," Ali Bhutto said to me.

"Are you sure of your army?" I asked him. "I have this intuition. I think you may get what you want, but I am afraid for you."

A short time later I heard there had been an army coup led by Zia ul-Haq. When Ali Bhutto was executed I felt dismal for his Iranian wife and his lovely daughter (who now lead his party). Yet I can still remember vividly that last conversation, as my friend sat behind his desk, very contained, with a cigar between his lips, slowly saying: "Yes, yes, I'm very sure of my army." Then he added: "Why, I took this chap [Zia ul-Haq] by the hand and brought him along to where he stands now."

The lasting souvenir I had from Ali Bhutto was my introduction to Chou En-lai. I had long held the conviction that a country of so many millions could not be ignored, and especially not by an organization like the UN. Ali Bhutto knew I wanted to meet Chou En-lai, and he arranged an introduction in Pakistan's Embassy in Indonesia.

This meeting led to my first trip to China, where I was assigned an armed guard, a small, delicate-looking girl (I found out later she was the niece of Mao Tse-tung) who went everywhere with me. Another constant companion was an ever-present translator. When I met Chou and spoke to him in French, he said to me; *"Je sais très, très peu français."* But I think even if he knew more than a little French, he would still have used an interpreter—it seems all the Communist countries follow this bit of protocol. I liked Chou En-lai very much, from our first meeting. He was soft-spoken, suave, a bit effeminate perhaps, and very gentle. He was a very learned man, the grandson of a mandarin, and during the talks and lunches we had together he would tell me stories about the traditions and customs of his country. In spite of his gentle manner, Chou had shown a remarkable gift for bouncing back; in fact he had been nicknamed "Pu-tao-wong," the Chinese name for the dolls that bounce into upright position no matter how you throw them down. He attended college in Japan, and as a student he was already a political activist, organizing leftist demonstrations. In 1919 he demonstrated against the Versailles Treaty and, like many Third World politicians, spent some time in jail.

In spite of their reputation for inscrutability, I found Chou En-lai and all the other Chinese political leaders I met rather frank and open. Unlike the Russians, who employ a great deal of verbal circumlocution in their political discussions, the Chinese will tell you precisely what they think and want—and they will expect you to do the same. Their political subtlety comes more into play in their aid programs to other countries, I think. Where the Russian presence in a nation is always very bold and rather aggressive, the Chinese tend to keep a low profile when they are "guests" in another country.

I was very interested in the kind of life led by the average Chinese worker, and since it's hard really to learn anything like this during the rounds of official visits, I stopped one day and walked into a house at random. It was very small but very clean and tidy, and although an entire family (from the grandmother to the youngest children) shared limited space, they seemed serene and at peace with their environment, as did most of the people I met.

When I returned home, I said to my brother: "You can't just ignore a country of 800 million people. You can't accept Taiwan as representing China and pretend that mainland China doesn't exist." Although he agreed, formal diplomatic relations between Iran and China were not established until 1974.

However, after I made my first visit to Peking, I maintained very cordial personal relations with China's political leaders. The last time I saw Chou En-lai, he was in a sanitorium, very thin and very tired, and I realized that this gentle and learned man would soon be gone.

During the years I lobbied for China's acceptance into the UN, I asked her leaders and diplomats if, when they became members of this world body, they would work to end the veto power. Although they have not done this, they have at least refrained from exercising this prerogative.

As a woman who is always preoccupied with work, I have allowed my personal life to drift, to take care of itself, as it were. Clearly this is not the kind of attitude that makes for terribly successful marriages. I had changed partners, I had gotten older—but I had not changed. After a very auspicious beginning, my third marriage too started to show signs of strain. In the first few years, my husband tried hard to adapt his life to fit my hectic schedule. He traveled everywhere with me, although he was involved in his own business affairs. In recent years, when he became interested in film production, he made the film *Caravans*, starring Anthony Quinn, Jennifer O'Neill and Behruz Vossojhi, Iran's most famous film star (who since the recent revolution fled the country—along with most of Iran's cultural and artistic community—and is now operating a filling station in California).

Soon, however, the kind of accommodation Mehdi had made in the beginning of our marriage became difficult to keep up indefinitely—and I respected him far too much ever to ask it of him. So gradually we started to lead separate lives, although we cared very deeply for each other, too much to make any kind of break. Instead, we have become very dear friends. Whenever it's possible, we spend time together—and when there is trouble, we know that we can call on each other.

This is almost the same kind of relationship I have with my children. I have insisted that they be educated—I wanted them to have the thing I had longed for most. But otherwise I have rarely invoked any kind of parental authority to keep them from making their own decisions.

The one occasion when I asserted my role as a mother precipitated a brief rift with my daughter Azadeh. I suppose I should have expected a negative reaction since she is very much like me and does not like to be told what to do. However, when at the age of twenty she fell madly in love with and married a man I thought was unsuitable, I couldn't keep silent. I reacted very badly, not so much because she defied me but because I knew how unhappy she was going to be, and I felt completely frustrated because she couldn't see what I saw. "You are my daughter," I said to her, "and you will always be my daughter, but for me this marriage doesn't exist. You are a grown woman, and you must make your own decisions, but I will not receive this man in my house."

After the marriage Azadeh and I saw very little of each other. We were both headstrong and stubborn and proud, and neither one of us was willing to give in. I knew she was reasonably well because I made inquiries through other family members (and I suspect she did the same).

Two years later, she appeared at my door, crying, with her baby son in her arms. "You were right, Mother," she said. "I understand you so much better now than I did before. I want to come home." I think we both understand each other better now, and when we talk, it is always as equals and as friends.

They have all been so different, my children. I have seen in them traces of me, of their fathers, of my father, of my brothers—shadings that colored their individual personalities.

My son Shahriar became a military man, just as he said he would. After graduating from the Royal Naval College, he joined the Persian navy and was stationed in the south. Although the climate there is blisteringly harsh, he loved the service. Since the navy was a relatively new branch of Iran's armed forces, all its officers were young men. Shahriar moved quickly through the ranks, and by the time he was 32, he was a commander. Under his direction, Iran developed a Hovercraft force, described as the largest in the world. He participated in the military action in the Persian Gulf area which resulted in the recovery of three islands, Abu Musa (from Sharjah) and the two Tunbs (from Ras al-Khaimah). When the revolution came, he was second in command of the naval base at Bandar Abbas.

My oldest son, Shahram, is completely different from his brother. When he finished his course in business administration at Harvard, he went directly into business for himself. He was very successful during Iran's "boom" period. (He would be envied by many, who would accuse him of using royal family connections to build his fortune. In 1971 he was subject to an unsuccessful kidnap attempt and even now he is still on the "enemies" list of the opposition.)

In recent years he has become something of a philosopher himself. Most of the year he lives quietly on a Seychelles island and devotes himself to various ecological causes such as saving endangered species. He has always had a calm, quiet nature, but now he has achieved a kind of peace and serenity that helps him to accept with equanimity whatever life offers.

# · VIII ·

# THE BEGINNING OF THE END

The Seventies marked another chapter in Iran's oil story. For Iran, oil has been a mixed blessing, not unlike great beauty for a woman: limited in duration (our reserves will probably be depleted by the end of the century), bringing problems, material gains—and exploitation by others.

For a long time my brother had felt that Iran could not formulate oil policies that were more for the convenience of the buyer than the producers. Long before American politicians took up the cry of "conservation," my brother had spoken of the need for developing alternate energy sources (in Iran we were experimenting with solar and nuclear energy) and for a reduction in the careless use of the world's resources.

Undoubtedly he antagonized many in the West when he pointed out that Iran had been selling oil cheaply and buying Western goods at a premium. To equalize this gap, he raised prices in 1973, from roughly $3 to about $12 per barrel. Internally this rise created repercussions, too; it led to a doubling of the national budget. No country can deal effec-

185

tively with this kind of phenomenon, especially a nation without a well-developed infrastructure and without the human resources to channel and administer this massive new infusion of funds. We had made tremendous strides in reducing our illiteracy rate, but we were still generations away from having a corps of well-trained technocrats.

This new oil money created a false sense of security, a feeling that all our problems were eminently soluble, that we could buy anything we needed. Enormous hopes were raised—by the administration itself—that within ten or fifteen years Iran would grow completely out of its underdeveloped status and into a thriving, prosperous modern nation, like Japan or West Germany.

I feel this might have happened eventually, but for the short run we experienced the same kind of growing pains faced by our suddenly rich Arab neighbors. Government agencies spent, and then spent some more, without coordination or careful long-range planning. Our ports became choked with ships waiting for weeks and months to be unloaded; in 1976 the government paid $400 million in surcharges for these delays. In a period of unparalleled wealth, we experienced not only bottlenecks, but shortages on the most basic level. Our port delays caused shortages of some foods and consumer goods; the new heavy demands on our power supply (which was not growing fast enough to keep abreast of this demand) created power shortages and brownouts.

Like many of our neighbors who had suffered under a have-not status for a long time, we were determined now to have the "best"—and to have it quickly—and this impatience was often reflected in a kind of schizophrenia, a loss of contact with reality. I remember, for example, a planning meeting during which we were discussing the establishment of new day-care centers for working mothers. Since Sweden was known to have some of the best and most advanced day-care facilities, we were using the Swedish model for our own centers. I listened to proposals of what kind of cribs we should buy, and then to a discussion of how much "balcony space" each crib should have. Then suddenly I was struck with the absurdity of what we were doing. "Look," I said, "we are talking about cribs and balcony space for children who have never slept in a crib before, who are accustomed to sharing sleeping space on a floor with their parents and brothers and sisters. We can't create an alien environment for these children without creating new problems for them." In the end, we built a modern new facility where each child slept on a comfortable mattress set on the floor.

In this atmosphere of conspicuous wealth and even more conspicuous consumption, the gap between rich and poor became more pronounced—and more dangerous to the stability of the regime. Teheran had multimillion-dollar sky-scrapers, residential districts lined with the palaces and villas of new millionaires, spacious boulevards filled with luxury cars. Yet we still had large numbers who lived in remote unreachable mountain villages, as well as the urban poor, living in shanties, whole families in one or two rooms, sometimes without electricity or running water. This kind of contrast exists everywhere (I have seen slums no better than ours a very short distance from the White House).

Now our per capita income had gone up from $176 in 1960 to $1,997 in 1976, and we had full employment; by 1977 Iran employed over a million expatriates to meet its growing labor needs. Yet now we lived in the era of mass media, a time when a man who had a job for the first time in his life was exposed to reports that there were others who had much more. Psychologically, our have-nots were a different breed from those who had lived 40 or 50 years before. The latter were fatalistic, perhaps resigned to the harsh reality that they had been born poor while others had been born to wealth. The poor of the current decade are more restless (understandably so), impatient for a greater share of the new prosperity—and ready to be radicalized by those who promise "more."

In a sense, we had, with our optimistic statements and our ambitious development plans, offered our people more than we could deliver. And if we did not deliver, it was not because were were detached or uncaring, but rather because we had failed to understand fully enough that sudden wealth cannot provide instant solutions to complex national problems.

Even a sophisticated, well-developed country like the United States, with generations of prosperity behind it, has not yet completely—to say the least—solved the problems of poverty and hunger within its borders. Yet the Western media, which had tremendous influence on our students abroad and on our intelligentsia, became increasingly sanctimonious and judgmental about the problems and mistakes of the Shah. At one point in the 1970's there were about 60 different European and American opposition periodicals which were mailed regularly to tens of thousands of Iranians living at home and abroad.

Some of these were amateur efforts, but others were well-financed, well-produced publications, funded by interests whose names appeared on no mastheads, whose motives were more self-serving than anything else. In the Middle East this kind of "cold war" is particularly effective, because in countries where an invulnerable father-like image is all important, a leader can be destroyed (or created) by an avalanche of propaganda. Nothing, in fact, can be more devastatingly destructive than a media campaign. Once it begins, there are almost no effective defenses: a positive image is vulnerable, easily lost, but a negative one is unshakable, almost impossible to recover from. Once launched, a media blitz is self-perpetuating. Once a leader has been depicted as a "tyrant," a "despot," or a "mass murderer" in the press of one or two countries, others will follow, and balanced reporting becomes harder to find.

The distorted picture of my brother in the press had me concerned for a long time. I knew from my own experience that as far as the media are concerned it is always open season on public figures; but my nature makes it difficult for me to ignore biased, inaccurate stories, especially when they go beyond gossip-column sensationalism to harmful political allegations.

As a member of the Royal Family and an active political figure, I have drawn my share of press attacks—attacks which seem ridiculous to those who know me, but which have been used nevertheless by those who would discredit the Shah's regime. For example, there have been accusations that I have been involved in opium traffic. Nothing could be further from the truth. The Imperial Organization for Social Service, which I founded, created some 300 medical centers for the treatment of addicts; and I have personally given lectures all over the world, from New York to India, condemning drug abuse and drug smuggling. Iran has also cooperated with the government of the United States in its programs against opium growing. When Richard Nixon visited Iran, he and my brother reached an agreement which would ban such cultivation in our country.

In 1972 my brother made an official visit to Europe, and in his entourage was Houshang Davallou, a Qajar prince. Prince Davallou was an opium smoker, and like other opium addicts, he could substitute opium pills when he was traveling. He had asked a friend of his to provide him with opium pills upon his arrival at Geneva Airport. Thirty-five grams of opium were passed, the police noticed this transaction, and Prince Davallou was arrested in the airport. In Europe, this incident made headlines. *La Suisse* and *La Tribune de Genève* hinted that I was involved—I should have realized that if there was a scandal involving Iranians, Ashraf Pahlavi had to be behind it.

Then in the March 5, 1972, issue, *Le Monde* dragged up further accusations about still another so-called airport incident: "People still remember the incident involving Princess Ashraf, the twin sister of the Shah, and her entanglement with customs officials at Geneva's Cointrin Airport in 1967. The customs officials found several kilograms of heroin in a suitcase carrying the label of Princess Ashraf. The Princess denied the ownership of the suitcase. The Shah came to his sister's assistance, and the case was settled very discreetly."

Although my brother felt I should ignore the article and avoid further publicity, I hired a lawyer and sued *Le Monde*. A Swiss lawyer in Geneva made an official request to the Swiss government, asking for an explanation of this incident. The Federal Council of Switzerland issued a statement, published in *Journal de Genève*, which said that no such incident was ever recorded in either police or customs files. The *Le Monde* trial lasted a few weeks. The court not only awarded me damages, but also required *Le Monde* to print my denial of its article and publish a statement of my lawsuit against it. (In January of 1979, the allegation that I was involved in the drug business was brought up again, this time in the *Washington Post*. But in February of 1979, the *Post* published a correction, which said: "The *Post* has no substantive evidence that these reports are true, and regrets their inclusion.")

This particular scandal was neatly cleared up, but unfortunately allegations like this linger long after the public has forgotten the details. While such attacks on my character became routine, I was not prepared for the terror that came with being the target of an assassination attempt. During the summer of 1976 I was staying with friends at my house in Juan des Pins. We began the evening at one of my favorite restaurants, a place called Felix, on La Croisette, the coast boulevard of Cannes. After dinner we went to the Palm Beach Casino at the other end of La Croisette Boulevard. It was almost 3:00 A.M. when we left. Because I am subject to motion sickness, I usually like to sit in the front of a car. I sat next to the driver and two other friends sat in the back. We turned the radio on, and we were all enjoying the music as we drove to within 3 kilometers of my house, where the road narrows to a single lane. Suddenly a black Peugeot passed us at full speed, then turned left and blocked the road.

Two armed men jumped out of the car and started shooting. Thinking very quickly, the driver pushed down on the accelerator and sped ahead. The big, heavy Rolls-Royce crashed into the back of the Peugeot. The driver put the car in reverse and rammed the Peugeot again, as the bullets kept coming. I hunched down on the floor of the car—for once I was grateful to be so small—but I could see that the driver had been shot in the arm. A moment later I heard a cry from the back; one of my friends had been shot, and blood was running from her eyes. Our driver kept ramming the Peugeot and eventually pushed it aside. We drove away at high speed, but we noticed a motorcycle following us.

We stopped at a little café called Pam Pam, where the driver ran in to ask the manager for help. He came back in a rage and said: "The bastard refused to call the police. He said, 'Go away, I don't want any trouble here.'" The injured woman was rushed to the hospital, and less than half an hour later I learned that she was dead.

The next day when I saw the car, I realized how miraculous my escape had been. A total of 14 bullets had been fired, and most of them had been lodged on the side where I had been sitting. I believed then more than ever—as my brother does—that an individual has a fixed "appointment with death," so to speak, that it will not come before or after this time.

Rumors flew after this attack: Members of the opposition in Parliament suggested that I had Mafia links and that this attack was perpetrated by underworld hit men. However, the attempt was so amateurish that I am sure it was the work of Iranian novices—no doubt hired by the opposition—none of whom thought to puncture the tires of my car and stop us from getting away.

As of 1980, more than three years later, the French police still made no arrests, but the incident itself was brought up and distorted—and given headlines again—shortly after Khomeini returned to Iran.

Unfortunately it is always scandal or the hint of it that makes the news. So much of what happened during the 37 years of my brother's reign was the result of hard, slow work by many dedicated public servants, and while the results were nothing short of miraculous to anyone who knew and understood Iran, this is not the stuff of which spectacular stories are made.

Our social work programs were on more than one occasion described as "primitive" in the Western press, which often failed to add that these efforts never existed before or that the conditions we worked under were crude in the extreme.

During my brother's reign, and especially after the growing oil revenues gave us the means to expand our efforts, we tried to bring as much progress as we could, even to the most outlying rural villages, with as little disruption of traditional values as possible.

I have mentioned the establishment of village tribunals, so that a mechanism of justice would be available to those who could not or would not travel to the cities. Similarly, we initiated a system of "mobile schools" to serve the children of the nomadic tribes, as well as medical teams to provide health care and such ancillary services as family planning.

In the cities, we tried to alleviate the conditions of the urban poor by offering assistance, including vocational training, that would help families to become self-sustaining instead of remaining chronically dependent. By the final years of my brother's reign we were giving this kind of assistance to some 9,000 families who did not have an employed head-of-household.

For almost two decades I divided my time between domestic social work and the international conferences and meetings connected with my work in the UN. I was, for example, Chairman of the UN preparatory committee for the International Women's Year conference held in Mexico City in 1975. I believe very strongly in this kind of international activity and the exchange of ideas generated, even though for the short run the results are sometimes disheartening. In Mexico City, for instance, I found that real dialogues among all the representatives were very rare. Clearly the needs of Third World women, for example, were of a much more fundamental and less sophisticated nature than those of Western women, and there seemed to be little patience and understanding of these differences. Western women were much more concerned with the refinements of emancipation—job discrimination and equal pay, for example—while Third World women were still struggling for such basic freedoms as the right to divorce and the right to have custody of their own children.

Even when there was agreement on resolutions, there was always the problem of implementation. One of the resolutions we did pass called for each nation to allot a percentage of its defense budget, the percentage that would be spent in one day, to help fight illiteracy. But only the governments of Iran and a few small African nations actually followed through on this.

Although I am not a very patient person, I did come to understand (as the lessons of years of experience taught me) that no matter how discouraging the immediate results of international work might be, we really have no choice but to persist. The world is really much too small to allow any nation to focus its attention on only its own problems and needs.

As the citizen of a country that had suffered invasion and exploitation, that had been relegated to "inferior" status by the greater powers of the world, I felt almost compelled to make contact with the people of other countries that had shared a similar history. I made many trips throughout Asia, Africa, and Latin America, to learn how their people coped with problems of hunger and illiteracy and the struggle for progress under the inexorable pressure of time. For me, these trips have provided some of the most rewarding moments of a long and checkered career.

It is still difficult to detail the dates and events that signaled "the beginning of the end." Revolutions can never be traced to single causes, no more than world wars or economic depressions can. They are born of a whole network of events and conditions. As I search over and over to understand what happened to Iran and to the Pahlavis, I can find a number of answers—no doubt more than others can—but still, of course, much eludes me.

The pieces that are clear, however, and those I feel must be enumerated here, start with my brother's attempts, after World War II, to build a viable social, economic, and political framework for Iran. We had believed, as our father did, that as Iran changed and moved into the age of technology, our people would outgrow the kind of primitive fundamentalism which the mullahs for centuries had been able to mobilize to serve their own ends.

On this assumption, my brother forged ahead in three vital areas. The first was the land reforms of the Fifties and Sixties. The second was the radical modernization program which, virtually overnight, affected every aspect of Iranian life. Third, was the sweeping emancipation of our women, who moved, as it were, thirteen centuries in the course of three decades.

But all of these advances were politically costly to the Shah's regime. For one thing, we seriously underestimated the resistance of the clergy and their hold over the masses. The taking of their landholdings generated active and undying hostility. This led them to see all modernization as a sacrifice of old values in exchange for those of the decadent and godless West. The mullahs never wavered in this opposition, and the final rift came in 1977, when the Government cut off their subsidies. To pay the clergy millions of dollars annually was seen as nothing more than a form of bribery. But this decision came at a high price politically: anti-Shah sermons were preached from then on in 11,000 mosques throughout the land. Curiously, SAVAK, the Shah's secret police—the supposedly all-seeing, all-knowing intelligence source—made no reports on the extent and manner in which the mullahs were now using the sanctity of the pulpit to undermine the throne.

This kind of failure to keep my brother informed was one of a number of ways in which, it seems clear to me, he was undone from within by some of his most trusted friends and advisers. For example, each day my brother met with Hussein Fardust (who served as head of Imperial Inspections, head of the Special Information Bureau, and second in command in SAVAK), the same Fardust of childhood, whose assignment was to gather, evaluate, and distill all intelligence reports and news dispatches. Fardust functioned as a kind of conduit for vital information on the highest level, which he delivered daily to my brother. Although my brother is always very reluctant to believe the worst of anyone, especially a man he treated like a brother, I am convinced that Fardust must have withheld vital information from the Shah and was, in fact, in active negotiation with Khomeini during the last years of the regime. I think the events following the revolution support my view: at a time when anyone remotely connected with the Shah was being summarily executed, Hussein Fardust remains alive and well, prospering under the new administration as one of the heads of SAVAMA (which is Khomeini's name for SAVAK).

This withholding of information, whether from incompetence or disloyalty, was crucial to the erosion of my brother's power, since it caused him to miscalculate the strength and breadth of the opposition. This miscalculation in fact is what kept him much less concerned than he should have been about his growing unpopularity in the press, at home and abroad. There were countless stories that smeared his character, and I felt they should have been answered.

But the Shah always seemed to feel that it was a mistake to dignify such distortions with answers. "It isn't necessary to pay attention to media stories," he said, "when we know the truth. The other leaders of the world know, too, what I am trying to do."

But I warned him—"These leaders may let you down."

In retrospect, I think this attitude was perhaps the most serious mistake my brother ever made, for the media today have become a formidable political tool, an active participant (rather than a passive observer) in the shaping of world events, and I believe that in his failure to speak for himself, he may have contributed to his own downfall.

By this I do not mean that he ignored the press. For example, the Shah was very aware of the newspaper stories that reported on corruption in Iran. Admittedly this was a serious problem and one not to be minimized, but historically it can be seen as an inevitable consequence of centralized bureaucracy (America's federal welfare system, which was meant to serve the people, has also led to similar bureaucratic abuses). Ironically, we had come full circle since the days when my father unified and pulled together a country of scattered provinces and rural villages. He had done this by bringing the administration of every town and village under the direct control of the Teheran government. But now, as my brother continued to work for centralization, he knew that once this was accomplished, that once the inhabitants of these villages thought of themselves as Iranians first and as Kurds or Baluchis or Azerbaijanis second, he would then have to relax Teheran's power and return some of it to local administrations. The Shah in fact had drawn up a blueprint for decentralization, not only as a way of controlling bureaucratic excesses, but also as a recognition of the ethnic diversity of Iran. Under this new system, he saw a series of workable checks and balances that would hold the central government in line while giving the people a voice in their local governments. Unfortunately, however, there was no time to implement this plan fully. The spiral of events that would end his reign forced the Shah to attempt instead a series of short-term, stopgap measures.

In the summer of 1977, he made moves to "clean house" and to reduce his control over the Government. To do so he felt he needed a new and more active Prime Minister, and on August 6, he dismissed Amir Abbas Hoveyda, who after 13 years had become less forceful and effective than he had been, and replaced him with Jamshid Amouzegar. He also barred government officials from taking part in business transactions that could in any way be considered a conflict of interest. A number of officials resigned at this time, no doubt choosing their business interests over service to the government. But these measures in no way stemmed the tide of unrest. Attacks in the press continued, the opposition mounted.

In November my brother went to America to meet with President Carter at the White House. He was frank with him about the seriousness of the troubles he was facing at home. It was Carter's assumption—the first in a long series of misdiagnoses—that what Iran was suffering from was still too much authoritarian rule and from reforms that, by

Western standards, had still not gone far enough. Carter was then in the midst of a campaign for world human rights (in part the result of the international furor over the Shcharansky case), and wanted to enhance his own image in this area. He therefore advised the Shah to accelerate liberalization policies, which was exactly what Iran did not need at the time.

One month later, as the year was coming to a close, President Carter and his wife, Rosalynn, came to Teheran—in what was at least a display of close friendship for Iran. We organized a gala New Year's Eve party for the Carters at the Niavaran Palace. It was a very festive affair. The First Lady was warm and cordial, although a bit more reserved than her husband. Carter danced with me often and insisted on having photographs of us taken together.

After midnight, in his first speech of 1978, the President drank to the health of the Shah. He spoke at length, and I quote from some of his remarks:

> I think it is a good harbinger of things to come—that we could close out this year and begin a new year with those in whom we have such great confidence and with whom we share such great responsibilities for the present and for the future....
>
> Iran, because of the great leadership of the Shah, is an island of stability in one of the more troubled areas of the world.
>
> This is a great tribute to you, Your Majesty, and to your leadership and to the respect and the admiration and love which your people give to you.
>
> We have no other nation on Earth... closer to us in planning for our mutual military security. We have no other nation with whom we have closer consultation on regional problems that concern us both. And there is no leader with whom I have a deeper sense of personal gratitude and personal friendship.

As he spoke, I looked at his pale face. I thought his smile was artificial, his eyes icy—and I hoped I could trust him. But within that very year he sent several emissaries to Khomeini, sent a military envoy to Teheran to undermine my brother's army, and hedged his own political bets by abandoning my brother as Iran moved toward revolution.

Less than a week after his departure, there were riots in Qum. And on February 18 there were serious riots in Tabriz, during which about 100 people were killed. Critics accused my brother of condoning this bloodshed, but they did so with little firsthand information of what the actual conditions are when troops are sent to restore order (even when those troops have been instructed to exercise restraint) among a howling mob that has been put into motion by professional agitators and terrorists, many of whom are armed and dangerous. In the heat and hysteria of the moment it is very difficult for the average soldier to differentiate between the unarmed civilian and the professional terrorist. Even in a highly civilized country like the United States, policemen have been known to shoot unarmed civilians and National Guardsmen have been known to kill unarmed students when they present themselves as a threatening mob. In a country like Iran, with a long history of political terror, with a history of agitators who have been trained and armed by outsiders, the massing of a mob cannot possibly be regarded in the same light as a demonstration in a country like the United States.

If my brother had indeed been willing to keep his throne at any price, I think he would have ordered a massive show of force at Tabriz and a severe curtailment of personal liberties—but he chose to do neither of these. After the Tabriz riot, I said to Prime Minister Amouzegar: "I think you must be careful that this doesn't snowball into something more serious." He seemed to feel that he had the situation well in hand. He was, of course, mistaken. Similar incidents followed, in Qum and Meshed and Teheran. These riots took place during a steady campaign of biased anti-Shah news reports by the BBC—almost a reprise of the attacks made on my father four decades earlier.

From France, where Ruhollah Khomeini had taken up residence at Neauphle-le-Château after Iraq expelled him, there came another barrage of "down with the Shah" speeches. From Germany and the United States, still more of the same. Once these attacks started, it was, as my brother said, "as if some mysterious orchestra leader had given the green light to this offensive."

Iranian students, at home and abroad, became a virulent fifth column directed against the throne. (At the beginning of my brother's reign, less than half a million students were enrolled in schools of all levels; by 1978 the number had gone to 10 million, with 185,000 in colleges and universities, 60,000 abroad. The tragic irony of how a half century of progress in education was destroyed by these students will become more evident as time goes by.)

Yet, despite what was clearly now counterindicated, America continued to pressure my brother to even further "liberalize" and "democratize" his regime—once again a Western solution to an Eastern problem. That this was a serious mistake became clear in August 1978 when the Shah announced that there would be free elections open to all parties the following spring. Within a week of the announcement there were riots in Isfahan, necessitating the declaration of martial law in that city. Two weeks later there was a terrible fire at the Rex Cinema in Abadan, a fire which killed 477 people and which was blamed on the government. In the political climate of a Western country, such a charge would probably not be given much credence, but in Iran it was widely circulated and very effective as anti-Shah propaganda.

On August 27 my brother appointed a new Prime Minister, Sharif Imami (again a move that was the result of American pressure), former President of the Senate and

Director of the Pahlavi Foundation. I heard about this appointment while I was attending a conference in Brazil, and I was astonished at the choice: I felt the situation called for a stronger leader.

Imami was given virtual control of the Government and began his administration by trying to appease everyone. From this point on it was almost as if the regime was committing suicide by degrees. To satisfy the religious right, he reinstated the Muslim calendar and closed nightclubs and casinos. But basically Imami was presented as the leader of a new policy of liberalization. For the first time in many years, the Prime Minister chose his cabinet without consultation with the Shah. For reasons best known to himself, the Prime Minister's cabinet included a number of former SAVAK men, at a time when the mere mention of SAVAK was like waving a red flag. Obviously the people had no way of knowing that the Shah had nothing to do with these choices. To make matters worse, the Prime Minister presented his cabinet to the Majlis (Parliament), invited free debate on this and other matters—and had all the proceedings televised. Charges of corruption flew, the cabinet was attacked, and the Prime Minister, in keeping with his concept of "democratization," thanked those who made the accusations. To the people who watched, this kind of display was confusing, to say the least. It was as if the Shah had declared an open season on the government. Virulent attacks appeared in the newspapers, criticizing everyone and everything connected with the government (the press was still free to do so). In the face of all this, the Prime Minister remained conciliatory, an attitude which, given the situation, could only aggravate the difficulties.

In a country like Iran people are drawn to power and strength. They demand a ruler who has a strong image, and not one who has been tainted with the mark of an appeaser. The Carter Administration's insistence on America's version of "human rights" had the opposite effect of what was intended: it signaled to the Shah's opponents that the United States had in effect made up its mind to abandon him. To give concessions in this atmosphere signaled a weakness born of desperation, rather than a genuine attempt to conciliate and heal. I feel that concessions should be made before people take to the streets, or after order has been restored, but most definitely not in the face of riots and disorder.

Even when Sharif Imami finally declared martial law in Teheran, he did so in a halfhearted and temporizing manner, as if he were afraid to let the people know what he had done. A friend of mine told me later that when she was discussing the curfew and other restrictions with her housekeeper, the woman said, "But madame, this doesn't apply to me; the curfew is only for terrorists, isn't it?"

Whether in ignorance of the martial law situation or in defiance of it, there followed on September 8, 1978, a huge and violent demonstration in Teheran. Government troops fired on the crowd, and 85 people were killed and about 200 wounded. The newspapers called this "Black Friday," and rumors raised the death toll to thousands. The effect of this day was tragic, not only because people were killed, but also because no attempt was made to keep order so that no other lives would be lost.

It was at the time of this extreme turbulence that I saw Iran for the last time. I had been in Russia attending a conference of the World Health Organization (WHO) in Alma-Ata, Kazakhestan. During the course of the meetings I made a request, through the usual diplomatic channels, for a meeting with Brezhnev. Relations between the Russians and Iran had been correct but cool, ever since China and Iran formed closer ties. (I had been outspoken in my support of this and of China's admission to the UN.) I had hoped for an informal talk with Brezhnev and for the opportunity to thaw my personal relations with the Russians.

My request for a meeting brought the kind of diplomatic

excuses that mean "no." Under normal circumstances the refusal might not have seemed particularly significant, but now, at a time when Moscow Radio had joined in the attacks on the Shah, when my brother was virtually besieged, every setback took on an ominous quality. Curiously, in the midst of this conference, I was invited to a dinner given by the American Ambassador. Seated next to me was Senator Edward Kennedy, and I remember our cordial talk. He inquired about the Shah and expressed his concern about the problems my brother was facing. He told me he hoped "everything will turn out well." (Incidentally, Senator Kennedy had been in Iran in the spring of 1975. He delivered a speech at Teheran University, in which he praised us for our remarkable achievements in the Middle East.)

I left Alma-Ata and flew to Teheran. As the plane flew me home, I remembered my last visit with Brezhnev—how gay the atmosphere had been during a banquet he gave for me. He was joking and laughing, as he usually did when he was not conducting official business, and when it was time for dessert, he began picking strawberries from a plate and popping them into the mouths of all the ladies present. When it was my turn, I accepted his offer with thanks, and he clapped his hands with delight.

Yet now I felt that no matter what was happening on the surface in my country, it was extremely likely the Communists were behind much of the disorders. I don't believe that ever since the days of the Imperial tsars Russia has altered one bit her desire for Iran's warm water ports. (Right now Brezhnev is maneuvering for a trade off: relaxation of Soviet domination of Afghanistan in return for all nations of the world having access to Middle East oil.) After the fall of Mossadegh I read a story in an American publication, written by a former Soviet secret agent, Lev Vasiliev. He described a meeting of top Soviet diplomats conducted by Russia's Ambassador Sadchukov in Teheran in January 1949. According to Vasiliev, Sadchukov said: "Comrades, something must be done about the Shah. So long as he lives, Iran will never go Communist."

"Then he must stop living," answered Christopher Oganessian, the Soviet Consul General.

This was the origin of the assassination attempt of February 1949. When this failed, the Russians embarked on a five-point program, said Vasiliev, a program which they have followed intermittently for the last 30 years. It called for "the infiltration of spies and traitors into every channel of Iranian life; bribing of every official who can be bought; blackmailing of those who can't; nationalization of Abadan refinery and other measures to disrupt Iranian economy; breakdown of law and order by campaign of terror, including riots and assassinations; propaganda of unparalleled viciousness through press, leaflets, and religious organs." On this last point, incidentally, Vasiliev described enormous sums being spent on the secret subsidizing of newspapers and magazines and on the establishment of close ties between Russia and many Iranian mullahs. "When these mullahs preach the 'Soviet party line,'" he added, "it has a great effect upon the devout Iranian Moslems."

How consistent the Russians have been, I thought, and how effective, especially in their use of a force the West has mistakenly assumed to be a strong bulwark against Communism—the religious right. Even now the Western press makes the mistaken assumption that there is such an entity as "an Islamic nation" that can be mobilized against Communism. They do not realize that pan-Islamism has historically surfaced as a form of reaction against outside domination, usually Western, that its most effective use is to prepare the way, not for religious, but for secular political movements.

The last of the recollections I had as my plane headed for Iran was of a conversation I had had with Khrushchev years before. He warned me that Iran had been unwise in its choice of the United States as a friend, that one day I would see the truth of his words. Later he expanded on this theme when he was talking to a group of reporters, saying that Iran was like an apple that one day, when it was ripe, would fall into the hands of the Soviets. At the time, the statement was strongly condemned in the Iranian press, but now the monarchy was in serious danger, and Khrushchev's words took on a strangely prophetic quality.

Iran and the monarchy had survived so many crises in 2,500 years, had revived from its nearly fatal malaise at the turn of the century—it seemed unthinkable that the country would fall now, and yet...

When I landed at Teheran's Mehrebad Airport, I had to face a grim reality. Mobs of people were demonstrating around the Shahyad Monument, and I was told that the roads were blocked, that I would have to use a helicopter to get to my house in Saadabad.

As I flew over the Shahyad Monument, I saw that one corner was completely dark. A moment later I realized this black mass was a mass of Iranian women, women who had achieved one of the highest levels of emancipation in the Middle East. Here they were in the mournful black *chador* their grandmothers had worn. My God, I thought, is this how it ends? To me it was a little like seeing a child you had nurtured suddenly sicken and die.

I reached home late in the afternoon. The following day I went to see my brother. He was, as always, completely calm on the surface, but I could see that he was extremely anxious.

"What will you do?" I asked. "How much danger is there?"

He did not give me a direct answer. Instead he said: "It is not wise for you to be here right now. You know how often you are made the object of attacks against the regime. I think you had better leave at once."

"I won't leave you alone," I argued. "As long as you are here, I'll stay with you."

For the first time in our adult lives, he raised his voice to me: "I am telling you that for my peace of mind, you must go."

So I left Iran and flew to New York, not knowing that it was the last time I would see my country.

There were new and more serious demonstrations in Teheran. The post and telegraph employees announced a strike, demanding more money and better housing. A representative of the Prime Minister promised a 40 percent pay rise, and the strikers went back to work. The next day, one after another of the ministries went out on strike, their employees all submitting photocopies of the original series of demands. When the Ministry of Finance joined the strikers, disorder compounded disorder when it was realized that no one on the government payroll would be paid.

At the end of October 1978, the employees of the oil industry went on strike, and production dropped abruptly from 5½ million barrels per day to 100,000 barrels per day. Since Iran's domestic consumption is 700,000 barrels per day—to fuel automobiles, furnaces, and even the ovens in which bread is baked—this particular strike, following the others, brought the economy to a grinding halt.

Within one year the cost of living went up 50 percent; for the first time in years Iranians were unemployed, and this after we had previously employed more than a million expatriate workers. Gas lines and shortages followed, and in this atmosphere of disruption and dislocation, "war of the cassettes" accelerated. This is the kind of propaganda move that has been quite effective in the Middle East: the mass distribution of tapes exhorting the people to take to the streets, to go on strike, to destroy the government—promising oil, money, and food as a reward for their efforts. It may be hard for a Westerner to imagine the hypnotic spell this kind of one-way communication could have on the masses, but it was considerable, especially during this period of

206

confusion and unrest. Loudspeakers were set up on roof-tops, and all during the night the messages came, sounding like the mullahs' exhortations to prayer, but instead calling for strikes and demonstrations.

The psychological effect on the masses gave an almost messianic quality to Khomeini's long-distance campaign from France. At one point the rumor was circulated that Khomeini's image would appear on the full moon, and thousands of people poured into the streets to see this miracle. Many swore that they did indeed see the image of the man who was being touted as Iran's savior.

Riots broke out in Teheran: shops, hotels, banks, public buildings, embassies were burned and/or looted. Prime Minister Imami resigned, and, on November 6, 1978, my brother appointed General Gholam Reza Azhari to form a military government. The country saw three days of relative peace as the people waited to see how "military" this military government would be. Then the testing began again. General Azhari released the last of Iran's political prisoners, who numbered no more than two or three hundred (about 1,200 had been freed in the months before) contrary to the inflated estimate of tens of thousands. Also, he repeated an offer that had been made before—amnesty to all Iranians who would respect the constitution—but the cycle of strikes and short-ages continued.

Throughout these developments, the British and Russian ambassadors gave my brother repeated assurances of support, but it was more lipservice than real support, so it hurt the monarchy more than it helped. Then in January 1979 my brother learned that General Robert Huyser, a Deputy Commander-in-Chief of the NATO Command in Europe, had been secretly visiting Teheran and that he had been in touch with Mehdi Bazargan, the man who briefly became the first Prime Minister under Khomeini. Although the Soviet press hinted that Huyser's secret visit presaged a military coup, we learned later that his mission was to neutralize and make ineffective Iran's army, to prevent the Shah from undertaking a military coup and to ease him off his throne. Among those with whom Huyser conferred: my brother's childhood friend, Hussein Fardust, and my brother's Chief of Staff, General Gharabaghi (although the Shah is reluctant to believe that those he trusts are capable of disloyalty, I had an intuitive mistrust of General Gharabaghi, and when my brother announced his appointment as Chief of Staff, I voiced my doubts and asked him to reconsider this choice).

As my brother sought politicians to form a coalition government that would represent and satisfy all the elements of the opposition, he found most of the men he approached reluctant even to discuss such a possibility. In Iranian political circles the feeling was that America had now clearly abandoned the Shah, and a great many politicians and military men (including Fardust and Gharabaghi) were so sure of this that they already made overtures to Khomeini.

Eight days after January 3, 1979, the day my brother named Dr. Shahpour Bakhtiar as Prime Minister, Cyrus Vance announced in Washington that the Shah was leaving Iran "for a brief vacation." (I later learned that during those eight days the leaders of America, France, Great Britain, and West Germany met at Guadaloupe and discussed the events in Iran; I believe it was decided then that the Shah would not return from this "vacation.") Bakhtiar's government did not have a chance: Khomeini had agreed to confer with Bakhtiar in France, but once Khomeini was assured that he had nothing to fear from the Americans (information from Iranian dissidents led the State Department to mistakenly believe that support of the Islamic right was the best way to stave off inroads by the Communists who mobilized the poor against the rich and the throne), Khomeini reversed himself and refused even to see Bakhtiar. He would soon return to Iran and set in motion the historical course we all now know but then never could have imagined.

## · IX ·

# EXILE

On January 16, 1979, my brother and his wife flew from Teheran to Aswan, the first stop of his flight into exile. It was announced on January 24 that Iran would become an Islamic Republic, and on February 1, Ruhollah Khomeini returned to Teheran. As the last Prime Minister appointed by the Shah, Bakhtiar was left completely isolated. He tried to call out the army to protect both himself and what was then the shreds of the remaining government, but General Gharabaghi had already "delivered" the army to Khomeini. Fearing for his life, Bakhtiar made a hasty departure by helicopter, and Khomeini named his own Prime Minister, Mehdi Bazargan.

I had followed all these events closely, and of course I was greatly concerned for the safety of my brother. As soon as he and Farah arrived in Aswan, I telephoned them. There were several very bad days when I didn't know what had happened to my son Shahriar. The press had published a report that he had been arrested, and I know that the revolutionary regime had decreed he be executed. Then there was no news at all. The waiting was agony, but then I

209

received a phone call from an Arab country in the Persian Gulf. It was Shahriar.

"I know you've heard about the arrest, but I had no way to reach you until now. It's a miracle that I'm alive, and I'll find a way to be with you soon."

I thanked God that he was well, and I listened as he told me how he had escaped. Somehow he had managed to get hold of a small pleasure boat with an engine. With a friend who was also a navy man, he had left Bandar Abbas. The waters there are very rough and difficult to navigate, and the two men had only a brief head start before the revolutionaries sent two boats to pursue them. Fortunately a severe storm, which threatened to overturn the small pleasure boat at any moment, also forced the pursuers to turn back. My son was safe, for a little while, but his friend decided to go back to Iran, where he was immediately arrested (and, no doubt, executed).

After his father's death, Shahriar and I had become closer, and we had an especially warm reunion. We talked for a long time about what might lie ahead for Iran. He told me that he couldn't bear the thought of living in exile, that he had sworn to return to Iran at any price. I was afraid for him, but I knew that if I were in his position I would be saying exactly the same words he spoke. He was so much like my father and my brother Ali Reza. He was an Iranian and a soldier, and he did not know how to be anything else.

I then went to Morocco, where my brother had gone after leaving Egypt. We were received by King Hassan with every kindness and hospitality. Although my brother appeared to be in reasonable health, he was acutely distressed by the news from home. It appeared that this man of God meant to found his Islamic Republic on a bloody purge of politicians, military men, journalists, teachers, businessmen, diplomats, professional people—anyone who had any part in Iranian life under the Pahlavis. And all the voices who had spoken so loudly about "human rights" in Iran were strangely silent. Museums, monuments, all the vestiges of Iran's monarchy were under attack, as if by sheer force of terror Iranians could be made to forget that they had lived under a monarchy for 2,500 years. Among the casualties that especially saddened my brother were the deaths of Amir Abbas Hoveyda, who had served as his Prime Minister for 13 years, and General Hassan Pakravan, the head of SAVAK—the same general who had saved Khomeini's life in 1963.

For me, the news of what was happening to Iran's women was extremely painful. After so many hard-won victories they were ordered to wear the veil again, were segregated and relegated to second-class status. At first Iran's women demonstrated against Khomeini's retrogressive edicts, and many were imprisoned or exiled. Those who continued to protest were faced by pro-Khomeini mobs of men brandishing knives and clubs. Feminists from Europe and America were appalled as they heard reports and even witnessed some of these scenes.

Not only women's rights, but any manifestation of refinement or civilization seemed to be prohibited under this new republic. During the early months of the regime a million and a half Iranians, including the intelligentsia and professional classes, left the country.

The Shah had intended his stay in Morocco to be indefinite (though not permanent), but late in April he was told he would have to leave rather quickly (within 24 hours) since his presence there was causing political problems for King Hassan. Finding a new home was difficult, and very stressful, since my brother had no wish to go where he was not wanted. The Shah's principal ally, the United States, and specifically the Carter Administration, apparently saw nothing wrong in officially ignoring my brother's plight, just a few short months after they had renewed their promises of support. Understandably, we turned to our personal friends for assistance, specifically former Secretary of State Kissinger and David Rockefeller (since the days of the Point Four

211

Program, when Nelson Rockefeller had been President Truman's Special Assistant on Foreign Affairs, the Rockefeller family had been close friends). When I read criticisms of these men because they were true friends at a time when it was neither socially fashionable nor politically expedient to associate with members of the Pahlavi family, I became angry at the blatant hypocrisy of those attacks. If the Shah was, as the press had suggested, so cruel and despotic a king, then the last eight American presidents should take their place beside him and share this so-called culpability, for it is a matter of record that America's leaders have publicly praised and supported the Shah's regime for almost four decades.

Failing to find official assistance in his search for a home in exile, my brother was able, with the help of personal friends, to make a temporary stop in the Bahamas and then to move to Cuernavaca. Here he was visited by former President Nixon, who had been a good friend since he was Vice-President under Eisenhower in 1953. I have met Richard Nixon only at formal receptions, so I never had the opportunity to know him well. But my brother has always felt that his grasp of international politics and his ability to formulate and sustain consistent foreign policy was superior to that of most American leaders. Unfortunately his achievements in this area—his termination of the Vietnam War and his normalization of relations with China—have been, as is well known, obscured by the Watergate issue.

Another visitor to Cuernavaca was former Secretary of State Henry Kissinger, a man I have known and admired since we met at a Washington reception years ago. Dr. Kissinger is an intellectual man, but also a man with a strong sense of reality—a man who realizes that power of the United States carries with it a moral responsibility to the rest of the free world. Although he has been criticized for his expressions of concern for my brother, it is clear that his actions on the Shah's behalf demonstrated a rare integrity, showing him to be a man whose moral commitments do not change with every shift of the political wind.

On a closer, more personal level, my brother has had the constant warmth and support of Queen Farah. Although this entire year of exile has been very harrowing for her, she has been steadfast in her courage and unwavering in her support of her family. I can see suffering in her face, but I have never heard her complain. For nearly twenty years she was a Royal Queen, but she has a nobility and strength of character that have nothing to do with either titles or circumstances.

For me, the consequences of exile have perhaps been less tumultuous than for other members of my family. I have been sent away from my country before, and I have lived much of my life among strangers. My political experiences have made me cynical about political friends, so I do not expect much of them, but I confess that these experiences did not quite prepare me for the behavior of people whom I thought of as personal friends, people whose previous warmth has frozen with "the first blast of slander."

The most difficult part of this exile has been to see and hear the proliferation of lies and accusations that have been heaped on my family. In the past I have more often than not ignored false stories about myself, regarding these to be part of the price of being a public figure. But now they seemed to me particularly insidious, since these unsubstantiated allegations are displacing the truth—and being presented to the public as so-called proof that the new regime in Iran is not as "bad" as the old one.

Later in the year, Fereydoun Hoveyda, former Iranian Ambassador to the UN and brother of the late Amir Abbas Hoveyda (who had been Prime Minister for 13 years), appeared on U.S. television and strongly criticized Kissinger for his defense of the Shah. In that interview, he painted his brother as a man who fought corruption in the Iranian Royal Family, and portrayed my brother as a despotic tyrant.

Although I understand that Mr. Hoveyda, like some Iranian exiles, has turned his loyalties, I feel I must comment on charges made by a man whom I probably know as well as anyone else. During the years that Amir Abbas Hoveyda was Minister of Finance in the cabinet of Prime Minister Mansour, his younger brother Fereydoun was a writer living in Paris. He was also receiving funds from the Iranian Oil Company to make a film on Teheran. Later, I approached him and asked if he would like to employ his writing talents on behalf of the government. He accepted, and it was at my suggestion (and against the advice of Ardeshir Zahedi, then Minister of Foreign Affairs) that Hoveyda returned to Iran after 18 years in Paris to take a post in the Ministry of Foreign Affairs. He became Deputy Minister of Foreign Affairs and eventually Iranian Ambassador to the United Nations.

During all the years he was employed by the regime, Hoveyda had nothing but praise for my brother. During the height of the unrest in Iran, Fereydoun Hoveyda was one of those who spoke to me often, criticizing my brother's attempts at conciliation and suggesting that the Shah should use the army to repress all opposition.

Certainly I can understand his grief and pain after the execution of his brother. In his place, I might well react in the same way. Several times I have tried to explain to him that the Shah offered his brother the chance to leave the country safely—among the choices he gave him was a post at the Embassy of Brussels.

I first learned of my brother's medical condition early in 1979, after he left Iran. Ever since we were children, I have always had a strong reaction, both physical and emotional, to the sight of his illness or pain. It is not really the possibility of death that preoccupies either one of us. As different as we are temperamentally, we share a kind of fatalism that makes us feel we will die when it is time for us to die.

What I react to is my brother's suffering, and although he never admits he is in pain, I saw, when I visited him in Mexico, that his condition had deteriorated. In mid-October the Shah's Mexican doctors advised him to seek specialized treatment not available in Mexico. Once again, our friends interceded with the American administration so the Shah could be admitted to New York Hospital for treatment. It has been suggested that his physical condition was deliberately exaggerated so that he might enter the United States—a lie I find particularly odious because my brother is a very proud man who would not be a party to such a deception.

My brother was in New York for 12 days before Khomeini's "students" seized the 50 American hostages that are still being held as I write this book. The delay suggests to me that the move was not so much a gesture of spontaneous indignation as a calculated and very deliberate political act designed to provide an international forum for Khomeini (the media's amplification of every word and gesture have rewarded his acts of piracy with an audience he never could have otherwise achieved) and to create a theatrical diversion from what was happening in Iran, away from the square mile surrounding the U.S. Embassy.

What Khomeini did not want the world to know is that during this year there has been the *de facto* establishment of a social and economic framework that is basically Commmunist, regardless of the "Islamic" label that has been pasted on this amalgam of factions (with religion the least important factor). By now it should be clear to everyone that Khomeini is not as much in charge as he claims to be; although his face dominates the street posters, others behind closed doors, direct the affairs of state. While Khomeini held the world's attention with his threats and ravings, banks and industries were being nationalized, private lands were expropriated, and tens of thousands of private home owners were forced to take in additional residents. In short, an atmosphere and framework for a Communist regime was created, with one fundamental difference: it did not label itself as such. But what we have seen is the most retrogressive kind of repression committed in the name of religion, including the execution of homosexuals for "crimes against God" and the killing of pregnant women accused of adultery. Those who know our religion and who practice it faithfully—people like Egypt's President Sadat—have spoken out against the "lunatic" from Qum, who in turn says: "It is necessary that blood should be spilled. The more Iran bleeds, the greater will be the victory of the revolution."

To divert public and press attention from its excesses, the new regime continues to raise charges that the Shah and the royal family have stolen vast sums from the Iranian people, yet it has not produced a single document that would substantiate any of these charges. They speak of billions transferred by the Shah to Swiss banks, while Swiss banking officials say that the sum total of *all* Iranian holdings there (not just the Pahlavis') amounts to several hundred million dollars at most. They charge that the Shah misappropriated funds from the Pahlavi Foundation, and these charges are often given credence in the same newspapers that praised the Shah's progressive philanthropy when he established the Foundation. From the time the Shah established the Foundation in 1958, he intended these funds to benefit the people of Iran, and to this end he turned over a substantial portion of his own money. Like similar Western foundations, the Pahlavi Foundation made investments—in banks, hotels, factories, etc.—to generate income. But unlike the administration of Western foundations, the administration of the Pahlavi Foundation was carried out by a special commission, with my brother retaining only a titular role, the role of honorary president. Foundation funds benefited Iranian students (by 1977, about 13,000 had received assistance for studies in Iran and abroad), schools (textbooks were translated, published, and distributed), religious institutions (mosques were refurbished and maintained), and Iranian workers (after real estate and rentals had soared in Teheran, the Foundation began the construction of subsidized housing). Every year the Foundation published an annual report and a financial statement in Iranian newspapers.

The new regime has yet to substantiate any of its allegations that the Shah somehow spirited away billions of dollars of Foundation funds. So, too, has it failed to document its charges of financial frauds committed by the Royal Family. It has pointed to bank documents showing that there were loans outstanding to members of the Shah's family—without mentioning that these were secured commercial loans connected with various business ventures, such as warehouses and cold storage plants, and that these businesses have since been confiscated by the new regime.

I have also been attacked for financial misconduct because I have participated in the administration of various organizations—the Women's Organization, the Institute for Illiteracy, and three universities—but no mention has been made of the fact that all of these organizations had an independent board of directors and separate accounting departments for the distribution of funds. Failing to find any tangible evidence of wrongdoing, the new regime has resorted to such theatricality as brandishing my personal belongings, including my nightgowns, on Iranian television—presumably these tokens of affluence are meant to prove decadence and depravity.

Politically, I can understand Khomeini's campaign to vilify my brother and his entire family in the eyes of the masses. Some of his slanders come from a personal hatred of the Pahlavis, but more important than this is the fact that he fears that the very existence of my brother as a ruler in exile will become a focal point of the opposition to his own regime. The strange brand of Shi'ism which he has invented as a rallying point for the masses is already beginning to show signs of weakness as a unifying factor. The diverse ethnic groups—the Baluchis, the Kurds, the Azerbaijanis—as well as the diverse political factions that had been held together by the monarchy, are already feeling the strain of a faltering "Islamic Republic." As yet, the opposition is unstructured, much of it scattered among various groups in exile. But any observer of Iranian history knows that opposition in exile can be politically dangerous. And so Khomeini tries to erase the evidence that Iran's monarchy even existed (his followers attempted at one point to destroy the ancient city of Persepolis, but were stopped by the villagers) and to discredit the surviving members of the Pahlavi family.

All this I can understand. So can I understand the attacks of an American politician like Senator Kennedy, who on more than one occasion spoke to me of my brother's regime in the most cordial terms—1980 is, after all, an election year, and a headline or two can always be useful in shoring up a flagging campaign.

What I find harder to comprehend is the behavior of a man like Secretary-General Kurt Waldheim, who suggested that charges against the Shah be tried before an international commission. But my response is: By what right and by what authority does the Secretary-General propose such a hearing? The UN is not and never has been a judicial body, and it seems to me that in making this kind of a response to the new regime's terror tactics, the UN is establishing some very dangerous precedents. To yield to the pressure created by the taking of hostages, by appeasing those who perpetrate such acts, is an act of moral as well as political weakness. To join in the attacks on the deposed leader of a country who was a founding member of the UN and who has wholeheartedly worked for and supported the organization is unconscionable.

While I understand that Kurt Waldheim would not wish to antagonize the new regime under such tense circumstances, it would seem to me that he has gone far beyond what prudence and any rational diplomacy call for. As a leader of the Iranian delegation, I worked with Mr. Waldheim for many years, and our ties were much closer than a boss–associate relationship. Officially and unofficially, he had nothing but words of admiration and praise for my brother's administration. To then propose, in the name of the UN, a commission to hear allegations against a ruler he called progressive and enlightened simply because his regime has gone under must, I think, lead smaller member nations to believe that the organization suffers periodically from moral bankruptcy as well as political impotence.

Fortunately, such attitudes do not reflect the thinking of the public, especially the American public. During my brother's hospitalization, thousands of letters of encouragement and support, couched in the warmest and most touching terms, nearly filled a hospital room. These letters came from people we never met, as well as from old acquaintances.

I, too, received many expressions of sympathy when, early in December 1979, my son Shahriar was brutally murdered by a Khomeini terrorist on a Paris street. It is a day I will never forget. My daughter Azadeh called me from Paris, and in a voice choked with tears and grief told me that my son had been shot. If I hadn't already been so numb with the accumulated shocks and tension of the past year, I think this news might have totally destroyed me.

Now, months later, this day still seems like a bad dream, something that did not really happen. Because in the past Shahriar and I had been separated for months at a time while he was on military duty in the south of Iran, I still cannot believe that I will never see him again. But as the days pass, the feeling of emptiness becomes greater, slowly and by degrees. As I grieve for him, for his young wife and his two children, I ask myself—who will answer for my son's death?

Perhaps my turn will come also, because those who killed my son know that as long as I live I will fight back in any way I can. This possibility I have long since accepted and I am not afraid. I do fear for my daughter, who speaks out against the new regime both privately and in the press. I ask her to be cautious, but she is a grown woman, as strong-willed and independent as I am, and I know that no matter what I advise, she will do whatever she feels she must do.

Next to my brother, I think she is the member of our family who suffers most from this exile, who feels most cut off from the country and culture she loved so much. When we talk, I feel I have little comfort or consolation to offer her for this sense of loss.

Her brother, my son, was killed because he, too, was the kind of patriot who would not live quietly in exile. He died on foreign soil, shot from behind by a lone assassin—not a soldier's death. But I will not bury him in a foreign land. I have had his body embalmed, and one day he will be buried in Iran, as he would have wished.

After my son's death, I went for comfort where I had always gone since childhood—to my brother. I flew to Lackland Air Force Base in Texas, where he stayed before he took up residence in Panama. The Texas weather was cold, rainy, and gray, as cold and harsh as life itself can be.

The personnel at the base were gracious and kind, but the atmosphere of the barracks where we stayed was rigidly military, the security measures very stringent. To see my brother there, a ruler without a country, living almost in a state of siege, was almost more than I could bear. No matter what he was feeling, he was still every inch a king in his behavior—serene, accepting, and radiating a quiet dignity that gives strength to all of us around him.

We talked for hours about what was happening in Iran and where the country might be a year from now. At this juncture, it seems that no matter who or what contributed to the Shah's downfall, the Communists will certainly be the principal beneficiaries. Another ever-present danger—one my father and brother had often discussed—is that Iran will disintegrate into a group of ethnic and provincial entities with virtually nothing but a small nucleus left of the centralized country we had worked to build.

We talked about our children and we reminisced about different times, times when we had different options. What if . . . I mused. What if we had listened to Stalin 30 years ago, if Iran had chosen our neighbors in the north instead of our neighbors in the west—what then? The price of such an alliance might indeed have been very high, but perhaps the people of Iran might not be in a country which is today in a state of economic disorder and in danger of disintegration. Of course, it was an exercise in speculation, an intellectual puzzle that has no answer.

I looked at my brother in the gray light of that Texas barracks, seeing in that sad, calm face 60 years of life, of triumphs and failures and caring. It was a reflection of my own life, of all I had loved most. As long as he was there, nothing could defeat me. For his sake I prayed that this would not be the last chapter of a story that began 60 years ago in a soldier's modest house in Teheran. For his sake and for the sake of Iran, I hope there will be more.

# APPENDIX

[Editor's Note: The following statements were presented to the United Nations by Ashraf Pahlavi.]

---

## UNITED NATIONS CENTRE FOR ECONOMIC AND SOCIAL INFORMATION

### HEADS OF STATE OF 60 NATIONS SIGN DECLARATION OF SUPPORT FOR INTERNATIONAL WOMEN'S YEAR, JANUARY 1975

---

Eight Majesties and 33 Presidents are among the Heads of State of some 60 nations who have signed a Declaration of Support for International Women's Year 1975.

The Declaration was presented to United Nations Secretary-General, Kurt Waldheim, at a ceremony in the Security Council in New York on 10 December 1974 by Princess Ashraf Pahlavi of Iran.

In his statement at the presentation, the Secretary-General said that International Women's Year represented the decision of the United Nations to bring to the attention of all Governments and all citizens the fact that serious inequities continued to exist in many parts of the world between men and women, particularly in the spheres of education and employment. He added that the question of women's rights was one of human justice, and said the problems required better utilization of the world's human resources.

223

*Text of Declaration*

The Declaration noted that:

> "The fundamental principle of the equality of rights of men and women has been proclaimed in the Charter of the United Nations as well as the Universal Declaration of Human Rights, and reaffirmed in other international covenants and instruments.

> "The United Nations in addition has repeatedly recognized, as in the International Conference on Human Rights, that peace cannot be maintained nor can economic and social progress be assured without the full participation of women alongside men in all fields.

> "Unfortunately, progress in this direction has been extremely slow and there is still a wide gap between accepted principles and established practices.

> "In the search to improve the quality of life which characterizes the modern world, one cannot separate the progress of women from their integration in development.

> "Our hope of seeing women become a new source of equilibrium and harmony in society is based on the elimination of traditional forms of segregation in the division of labour in general.

> "We earnestly hope that on the occasion of International Women's Year, which is to begin on 1 January 1975, all States will consider taking concrete measures to this end."

Among nations represented by the signatories were: Afghanistan, Algeria, Austria, Australia, Bahrain, Bangladesh, Belgium, Brazil, Bulgaria, Canada, Cuba, Denmark, Egypt, Ethiopia, Finland, France, German Democrat Republic, Federal Republic of Germany, Greece, Hungary, Iceland, India, Indonesia, Iran, Italy, Ivory Coast, Lebanon, Japan, Mali, Malaysia, Malta, Mauritania, Mexico, Morocco, The Netherlands, New Zealand, Nepal, Norway, Nicaragua, Oman, Poland, Pakistan, Philippines, Singapore, Romania, Spain, Sweden, Sudan, Syria, Trinidad and Tobago, Turkey, United Kingdom, United States, Union of Soviet Socialist Republics, Uruguay, Venezuela and Yugoslavia.

# UNITED NATIONS ECONOMIC AND SOCIAL COUNCIL

CONSULTATIVE COMMITTEE FOR
THE WORLD CONFERENCE OF THE
INTERNATIONAL WOMEN'S YEAR
3-14 MARCH 1975

STATEMENT MADE BY H.I.H. PRINCESS ASHRAF PAHLAVI (IRAN),
CHAIRMAN OF THE CONSULTATIVE COMMITTEE FOR THE
WORLD CONFERENCE OF THE INTERNATIONAL WOMEN'S YEAR

In accordance with the decision taken by the Consultative Committee at its second meeting on 4 March 1975, the statement made by the Chairman at the Committee's first meeting on 3 March is circulated herewith.

In making me Chairman of this Consultative Committee, you have not only shown your trust, which touches me deeply and merits my sincere gratitude, but, more important, you have given me a task of whose magnitude I am fully aware.

In the history of the struggle for equality between men and women, proclaimed in the Charter of the United Nations and many international instruments, the role of our Committee may be decisive.

The Declaration on the Elimination of Discrimination against Women recognizes that such discrimination is fundamentally unjust and constitutes an offence against human dignity.

Unfortunately, despite all the efforts of international, regional and national bodies, this equality has remained largely theoretical.

Even today, discrimination very often begins from the cradle and accompanies women throughout life. In almost every private and public sphere women are often treated as inferior and marginal.

Whether within the family, at school or at work, to be born a woman is to be handicapped in some way. Not only is this situation extremely unjust and contrary to fundamental human rights and human dignity, but its harmful repercussions also affect men and children just as much as women and severely hamper the social and economic progress of mankind.

It was in order to give new impetus to action in this sphere, to mobilize international opinion and to induce Governments to turn their attention to this problem that the United Nations General Assembly proclaimed 1975 as International Women's Year.

In this year of 1975 the major event will undoubtedly be the Conference of the International Women's Year, the first world meeting to be devoted to the subject at the level of government delegations.

As you know, the main task of the Conference will be to draw up an international plan of action for making the central theme of International Women's Year, "Equality, Development and Peace", a reality; it is for the purpose of preparing this plan of action that this Consultative Committee is meeting today.

Accordingly, the success of the Mexico Conference will depend largely on the quality of our work, and its outcome will, in turn, determine the success of any future action on behalf of women.

Although there are some similarities in the problems of women throughout the world, the form they take varies a great deal from region to region. The fact that all geographical regions are represented within this Committee should enable us to keep this diversity of circumstances in mind and to deal with the overall problem.

Nevertheless, certain principles and basic data are common to all women throughout the world. This is so primarily because women's problem is a fundamentally human problem, it involves justice and respect for the human person as such. Justice and a sense of dignity demand that every woman should have equal opportunities, rights and obligations, towards herself as an individual, towards her children as a parent, towards society as a citizen.

The theme of equality is, of course, not new, and in this sphere the Commission on the Status of Women, in particular, has remarkable achievements at the legal level to its credit. Regrettably, the international conventions adopted have not been widely ratified, and moreover, even when the terms of a law are not discriminatory, it is not necessarily obeyed in practice.

In our times, open and legal discrimination may not be the chief obstacle to the advancement of women. The major problems arise, rather, from traditional attitudes to the role of women in society.

In this connection, a whole process of education and of changing the mental attitudes, not only of men but also of women themselves, is required, a long-term task which demands sustained and continuous effort.

It is not sufficient to proclaim great principles or to make fine declarations. The status of women will not be helped by verbal ectoplasms.

The true emancipation of women begins only with their economic independence. To give them the intellectual and technical equipment to earn their living directly, without depending on men, is to lay the foundations for their liberation.

It is in this sense that the integration of women in development is of real importance. There is a small but essential difference between the integration of women in development as a means of securing the advancement of women and the integration of women as units of labour, which, if considered from that viewpoint alone, could lead to increased exploitation.

Women's right to work on completely equal terms with men, recognition of the value of their contribution to society, within the home or outside it, this is the keystone of all action on behalf of women, and from it arise most of their other rights and obligations. The right to work in itself implies access to the practical means of *exercising* this right, namely, education and technical and vocational training, the abolition of the division of work into "male" and "female" sectors, equal pay for equal time and quality of work, the same career prospects and the same access to posts of responsibility, etc.

This implies, in short, the liberation of women from the chains which have so long confined them to the home. It is obvious that women cannot hope to participate fully in decision-making and in the economic activities of society until they are in a position freely to decide the number of their children. A high birth-rate, because of the servitude it creates, is very frequently accompanied by the attribution of inferior status to women and is as much the result as the cause of underdevelopment, a vicious circle which must now be broken.

In this sphere, as in all others, the fundamental interdependence between the status of women and the level of a country's economic and social progress is clearly evident.

That the international community seems to have become aware of this interdependence is evidenced by the Strategy for the

227

Second Development Decade, the Population Conference, the Food Conference and all the regional plans of action for the integration of women in development.

Basic to any action is the fundamental need for a policy of education. This education is required at several levels, and most of all in educating and informing the masses, to whom the role of women, all too often overlooked, must be made clear.

From their earliest years children hear that women are endowed with limited intelligence, less capacity for work, and a certain image of women within the home is inculcated in them.

Facts demonstrate the absurdity of these prejudices, but customs and traditions are such that women themselves often acquiesce in an image from which they are the worst sufferers.

In this sphere the role of communications and teaching programmes is essential.

Just as decisive are the struggle against illiteracy, and technical and vocational education for women.

Statistics show that the highest percentage of illiteracy is found among women. Even when primary education is compulsory, girls abandon their studies earlier and the percentage of their participation declines rapidly at the secondary level and falls very low at the technical and university levels. This is due to the fact that girls are accustomed to marry earlier and to confine their activities to household work.

Thus, women who want to work or who are compelled to earn their livelihood are everywhere faced with the same obstacles because of their lack of training. This resistance of societies to the education of women and to their participation in social and professional activities is based mainly on two mistaken ideas:

Firstly, there is the idea that children are the sole responsibility of the mother. However, since maternity is essentially a social function, simple logic requires that domestic and family responsibilities are shared equally among men and women. There is also the idea that the participation of women in the economic activity of a country is hardly necessary. However, in the first place, quite apart from any consideration of usefulness, the right to work is a fundamental human right, a source of development, freedom and independence.

Furthermore, it is well known that, in addition to their household tasks and their maternal duties, women in rural areas are responsible for a large and perhaps the major part of agricultural work.

In towns also, more and more women are compelled to work in order to supplement the family income; they thus have two jobs, one outside and the other at home, where the tasks are not shared to any great extent by the husband.

Finally, the marginal character of women's role in national economic development causes an enormous waste of human resources.

It is also obvious that the lack of education of the mother automatically affects the children in her care.

An oriental proverb rightly states: "Educate a man and you educate a person; educate a woman and *you educate a nation.*"

But it is not enough to educate; education as now conceived must be entirely reformed both in its spirit and in its methods.

While discrimination against women exists in nearly all countries and must be condemned as such, it is particularly evident in the poor countries where such vital needs as hygiene, food, housing, literacy and basic education are deficient at all levels. Moreover, the problems facing women in rural areas are different from the problems facing women in urban areas.

Our Committee must take all these questions into account in preparing a plan of international action.

The failures of the past must not discourage us; we can build only in a spirit of optimism and the year 1975 provides us with a solid basis for further action. Not only has the ground been prepared to some extent by the efforts of the last 30 years, but also it seems that for some time now Governments have become increasingly aware of the importance of the problem.

Of course, we cannot do everything at once in a field so complex as this—the plan of action which we must ponder can hardly be restricted to a period of one year, and we must admit that at least a decade of sustained efforts will be necessary to achieve substantial results.

Another reason for optimism lies in the fact that within a few months of the Mexico Conference, nearly two thirds of the Heads of State and Government of the world have approved the Declaration on International Women's Year which I had the honour to bring to their attention. In doing so, they have expressed their support for any specific measure designed to eliminate any form of discrimination against women.

For the international community, International Women's Year is a unique opportunity for promoting equality between men and women, not only in law but also in everyday life, ensuring the full participation of women in the development effort both at the planning and executing level, and guaranteeing them the full enjoyment of human rights.

There is no question of granting rights to women but of recognizing and respecting what is inherent in them, as human beings.

Moreover, harmony between nations cannot be guaranteed as long as harmony does not exist between men and women within each family, each enterprise and each country. Women have their role to play in peace-keeping, a role which no one can afford to disregard. As early as 1846, a great writer, Gogol, wrote:

> "The influence of women may be considerable, in particular nowadays, in the present order or disorder of our society, where we perceive a certain civic lassitude and a spiritual coldness, a kind of decline in moral values, which make an awakening necessary. To bring about this awakening, the collaboration of women is essential."

And, according to Oscar Wilde, the past can always be effaced, but the future is unavoidable.

It is high time to break once and for all with a past full of frustration and full of the exploitation of women and to begin a sincere drive towards a future where men and women will live in mutual comprehension, freedom and dignity.

Allow me to say a few words about the organization of our work.

We have only 10 working days to complete our task. We must therefore work constructively and with a certain discipline.

With that in mind, I would request you to limit your statements as much as possible.

I would also like to appeal to you to begin our meetings punctually and thus to avoid wasting time.

Before concluding, I would like to convey a special word of thanks to Mrs. Helvi Sipila, whose devotion and efficiency we have always profoundly admired.

Every day of this year of 1975 reveals to us more and more clearly that the choice of Mrs. Sipila as Secretary-General of the International Women's Year is an important factor in the success of our work.

In my individual capacity and in my capacity as Chairman, I

wish to express my gratitude to Mrs. Sipila and to pledge her our full support in the pursuit of her noble task.

I would also like to thank the members of the Secretariat, and Mrs. Bruce in particular, who, as can be seen from the excellent document submitted to the Consultative Committee, have brilliantly performed a very difficult task.

# INDEX